Welcome to
iPad
The Complete Manual

The iPad's impressive battery life, multi-tasking abilities and stunning high-resolution screen have revolutionised the way we carry out our everyday tasks. And since the introduction of the iPad mini, it's been even easier to complete these tasks on the go. But while the hardware is incredible, it's the apps that have made the iPad a huge success. And it's these apps that The Complete Manual focuses on. We take you through the iPad's best built-in apps, and show you how you can use them to benefit your life, whatever iPad model you own. Enjoy the book.

iPad
The Complete Manual

Imagine Publishing Ltd
Richmond House
33 Richmond Hill
Bournemouth
Dorset BH2 6EZ
☎ +44 (0) 1202 586200
Website: www.imagine-publishing.co.uk
Twitter: @Books_Imagine
Facebook: www.facebook.com/ImagineBookazines

Head of Publishing
Aaron Asadi

Head of Design
Ross Andrews

Production Editor
Gavin Thomas

Senior Art Editor
Greg Whitaker

Design
Perry Wardell-Wicks

Printed by
William Gibbons, 26 Planetary Road, Willenhall, West Midlands, WV13 3XT

Distributed in the UK & Eire by
Imagine Publishing Ltd, www.imagineshop.co.uk. Tel 01202 586200

Distributed in Australia by
Gordon & Gotch, Equinox Centre, 18 Rodborough Road, Frenchs Forest,
NSW 2086. Tel + 61 2 9972 8800

Distributed in the Rest of the World by
Marketforce, Blue Fin Building, 110 Southwark Street, London, SE1 0SU

iPad The Complete Manual Revised Edition © 2013 Imagine Publishing Ltd

ISBN 978-1909372740

Part of the

iCreate
bookazine series

IMAGINE
PUBLISHING

Contents

What you can find inside this bookazine

Find out how to purchase and download all kinds of apps from the App Store on page 40

Find your way around in Maps

Suitable for iPad and iPad mini

iPad mini
Every inch an iPad.

Browse the internet in the Safari app

140 **iPhoto**
An advanced editing app
• Organise photos • Apply swatch effects
• Use multi-touch editing • Share pictures
• Brush on adjustments • Make journals

An introduction to iPad

What makes the iPad one of the best tablets available? It's time to find out…

The original iPad completely transformed the tablet market. Its beautiful screen, portability and fantastic built-in apps struck a chord with consumers and critics alike. It is built to run iOS, the operating system also used in the equally as impressive iPhone and iPod touch, and so the general performance is as smooth as you could wish for. With finger-friendly icons and an environment that lets you get on with what you want to do, ease of use is apparent in every part of the software.

When you also consider the long battery life, exceptional build quality and near-perfect screen, you start to realise that this is a tablet built for anyone who wants to work and play anywhere. Thousands of apps are available to extend the experience as well and help you to get as much use as possible from one of the best tablets money can buy.

Fig 1 The simplistic Calendar app interface actually works well for complex agenda management

Get organised

The iPad is packed full of useful functionality out of the box and the tools to get yourself organised are all included. First up is the Calendar app, which looks quite basic at first glance, but when you dig below the surface you start to realise that the simplistic interface is actually very useful when handling complex calendars (Fig 1). You can deal with more than one calendar at once and also accept invitations automatically.

The Reminders app lets you quickly add tasks that need to be done at a certain time and alerts will sound when required. You can even set Reminders to activate when you reach a particular location. The Clock app will wake you up with an alarm every day and also includes timers that can be used for time-dependent tasks (Fig 2). We shouldn't forget the Contacts app which will help you to detail every person you need and to add lots of information for each one.

Fig 2 The Clock app can deal with alarms, world times and instant timings

Get work done

The iPad is not just designed for home use; it can be utilised for work as well. The Mail app is able to let you preview Office documents when they are received and you can also use the extra

screen size and well thought-out keyboard for writing things down using the Notes app. You can also utilise the Maps app to help you get to meetings and to plan ahead so that you understand how much travelling time you can expect.

As time has passed, the potential of the iPad in the workplace has been realised and there are thousands of apps available to let you undertake specific tasks. However, for the basics and the general day-to-day work tasks that take up most of your time, the iPad is able, from a software and hardware perspective, to help you get everything done that you need to.

Fig 3 The battery allows hours of great quality video playback. Perfect for those long flights

Enjoy yourself

The iPad is perfect for keeping yourself and your family entertained anywhere. The Video app lets you watch movies for hours at a time before a charge is needed, perfect for long distance flights, and the audio quality is superb through headphones and even the external speaker (Fig 3). The inclusion of iTunes takes your entertainment options to a whole new level (Fig 4). From music to movies and from TV shows to iBooks, everything you need is available to purchase and download straight to the iPad without the need for

Fig 4 Music, films, audiobooks, TV shows – they are all available to buy through the iTunes app

An introduction to iPad

How the iPad can improve your life

Productivity
The iWork suite of apps let you produce spreadsheets, presentations and documents easily and the touch interface makes work fun.

Lifestyle
Whether you want to improve your photos, make beautiful music or create home videos, you can do it all in style on an iPad using the iLife suite of apps.

Entertainment
The free iBooks reader lets you purchase and read ebooks that look like paper titles, and you can also watch full-screen videos and play music whenever you want to.

There are many situations where the iPad is perfect for providing entertainment

a PC. You can also create your own keepsakes using the camera or by transferring a photo collection to the iPad for viewing whenever you want to remember a good time. There are many situations where the iPad is perfect for providing entertainment and whether you want to simply read a book in bed or keep the kids amused on holiday, it is a great tool for keeping everyone happy.

Keep in touch
The iPad, whether it is a Wi-Fi-only model or mobile network capable, is able to let you connect, in a variety of ways, to those who are important to you. FaceTime lets you speak to friends and family thousands of miles away and the quality of the video stream brings

iPad accessories

Smart cases
iPads don't like being dropped, so a case will help you to ensure that your investment lasts. Cases like the Smart Case also add extra functionality that is extremely useful

Real keyboards
You can supplement an iPad with a case that contains a real keyboard, connecting via Bluetooth, like this Logitech case

Lightning to 30-pin Adaptor
This adaptor will let you connect a huge range of accessories designed for previous generation iPads to the latest versions, which will open up the number of accessories you can use

Mobile chargers
Mobile chargers offer the ability to top-up your iPad battery when travelling. This can be useful if you are on holiday or have no access to power

Speaker docks
A good quality speaker dock can turn your iPad into a home entertainment system that offers superb sound. It's also flexible and able to be used anywhere

Headphones
iPads are capable of providing very good quality sound, but the addition of a high-end set of headphones, like these Sennheisers, will improve the sound quality even further

Fig 5 Siri enables you to give instructions vocally and hear the results without any typing at all

everything to life. iMessage works like standard instant messaging, but it is completely free and will work across multiple devices, including Macs, so that you can keep the conversation going all of the time. You will also be notified when new messages arrive.

Of course there is a capable email app included and the ability to access multiple social networks via the Safari app or through third-party solutions is also open to you. Since the release of iOS 6, iPad users have also enjoyed the ability to ask their device questions and assign it tasks, such as sending messages, by using the Siri service (Fig 5). So you can even use your iPad to connect with other people using only the power of your voice – now that's progress.

Top iPad applications

Kindle
Get access to thousands of ebooks that are often well priced and start reading them in seconds on your iPad.

Tweetbot for Twitter
Regarded by many to be the best Twitter client available. It's beautifully designed and packed with features.

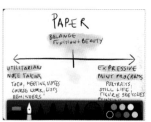

Paper by FiftyThree
This drawing app feels like real paper and anyone, regardless of talent, can create beautiful drawings.

Instapaper
This is designed to let you quickly save long web articles to read when you have some spare time.

Flipboard
This brings together social network feeds and news articles and presents them in your own unique paper.

Real Racing 3
Thanks to stunning graphics and adrenaline-filled gameplay, this is a racing game to let off steam with.

Amazon Windowshop
Go finger-shopping through thousands of products so that you make purchases quickly and easily.

Snapseed
With multiple filters and much flexibility, this editing suite is ideal for perfecting all of your photos.

WolframAlpha
For the curious of mind, this is like an app-based Wikipedia, but with more depth in the info it provides.

You can even use your iPad to connect with other people using only the power of your voice – now that's progress

Set up your iPad

We show you how to activate your iPad for the first time and familiarise yourself with this wonderful device

1 Turn your iPad on To turn on your iPad for the first time, press and hold the On/Off button (the lozenge-shaped button on the top right of the tablet) for about three seconds. If your iPad is new or has been recently reset you should be greeted with the Apple logo and then, after ten seconds or so (the time may vary depending on your model), a plain screen with 'iPad' written on it (Fig 1).

2 Resetting a pre-owned iPad If, when you turn your iPad on via the On/Off button, you are taken straight to the Home Screen, then your iPad is already activated. If you wish to reset the iPad so you can set it up as new, go to the Settings app and scroll down to the Reset option and Erase All Contents And Settings. You can then follow this tutorial to activate your iPad as new.

3 Slide to unlock At the plain-looking iPad screen (as shown in Fig 1), you need to slide your finger to the right across the arrow at the bottom of the screen to continue. At this screen the iPad is locked (as shown by the padlock icon in the top-centre of the screen). You will need to perform the sliding motion every time you wish to wake the iPad up, so get used to it!

4 Waking up the iPad If at any point during the activation process the iPad goes to 'sleep' (the screen goes blank), usually because it was left unattended, you can wake it up simply by pressing the Home button (the circular one at the bottom-centre of the iPad's front) or tapping the On/Off button (don't hold it). You'll then have to unlock your iPad as shown in Step 3.

5 Select your language Once you've unlocked your iPad, you will see a short list of common languages to choose from. If the language that you'd like is not in this list, tap the downwards arrow. You will then be presented with a long list of different languages (Fig 2). The language you choose here will be the language that your device is set to. Tap the blue and white arrow in the top-right corner.

6 Select your Country or Region Now, similar to choosing your language, you will have a short list of countries/regions to choose from (Fig 3). If your country or region is not in the list, tap 'Show More...' and pick yours from there. This will determine the apps that are available in the App Store and the various media available from the iTunes app, as well as the correct currency.

Fig 1, Turn on **Fire up your brand new iPad**

Fig 2, Select language **Choose from the list**

Fig 3, Select your region **This affects apps**

Slide your finger along the slider at the bottom of the screen to unlock your iPad

Set up your iPad

Fig 4, Location Services **This is used by apps**

Fig 5, Connect to Wi-Fi **Scan for networks**

Fig 6, Set Up iPad **Choose an option**

7 Location Services The next part of the process is dedicated to your device's Location Services (Fig 4). This allows apps to gather and use data indicating your approximate location, which is incredibly useful if you ever lose your device. For a more detailed explanation on the service, tap 'What is Location Services?' towards the bottom of the screen. Tap 'Done' when you've finished.

8 Enable or Disable You must either enable or disable the Location Services service by tapping on your chosen option – there is no option to skip the step. If you are still unsure of the purpose of this feature and need more information then don't worry; you can activate it later from the Settings app in the Home Screen. Tap 'Next' to continue the activation process.

9 Connect to a Wi-Fi network Your iPad will be able to connect to the internet wirelessly via a Wi-Fi connection. If you have a Wi-Fi network set up in your house it will appear in the menu (Fig 5). Tap on it and you will need to enter your password using the on-screen keyboard. When you've entered the password, tap the Join button either on the keyboard or the dialog box.

10 If you don't have a Wi-Fi connection… If you can't access a Wi-Fi connection, but you do have a computer with iTunes installed, you can continue the activation by connecting your iPad to the computer via the supplied USB cable and then choosing the 'Connect to iTunes' option beneath any other wireless networks the iPad could pick up.

11 Set Up iPad The next screen you'll see will present you with three options: Set Up as New iPad, Restore from iCloud Backup, and Restore from iTunes Backup (Fig 6). You will most likely want to choose the first option, which requires no more than a tap of the 'Next' button in the top right to continue with the activation (Step 14). However, we will also look at the other choices…

12 Restore from iCloud Backup You should choose this option if you have an iCloud account that has a backup attached to it. Once you've chosen and tapped 'Next' you'll have to enter the Apple ID of the account that has the backup, and its password. You'll then be able to restore the iPad from the backup. New iPad owners won't use this.

You can also activate your iPad via iTunes by connecting it to a computer via USB

13 **Restore from iTunes Backup** If you choose this option you'll be able to restore your iPad from a backup kept on your desktop computer in iTunes. Connect your iPad to your computer via the USB cable and select the backup you want to use from iTunes. Note that you can also set the iPad as a new one (as if you tapped the 'Set Up as New iPad' button in Step 11) from here.

14 **Apple ID** The Apple ID, which you create in the next step of the activation, is one of the most important things you will do during the process. A tap of the 'What is an Apple ID?' link at the bottom of the screen tells you why ownership of an Apple ID is essential. You will need one to download apps from the App Store, buy songs from iTunes and purchase books from iBooks.

15 **Create an Apple ID** If you have yet to create an Apple ID, it's incredibly simple to do so, and you do can do it from the comfort of your iPad. Tap the Create A Free Apple ID button (Fig 7) and you'll have to enter your birthday (which will be used in case you forget your password), your name, and the email address that will eventually become your Apple ID.

Fig 7 , Apple ID **You need one of these**

16 **Sign In with an Apple ID** Due to the exceptional success of Apple programs like iTunes, you may already have an Apple ID without so much as touching an iPad, Mac, iPhone, or iPod. If you have one, tap Sign In with an Apple ID and enter your ID and password. If you know you own one but can't remember the details, tap 'Forgot Apple ID or Password?' and you'll be able to retrieve it.

17 **Read the Terms & Conditions** After signing in with either your brand new or existing Apple ID, you will be presented with a screen of Terms and Conditions that relate to all aspects of your iPad and the services that you will be using, such as iCloud, Game Center and so on. If you wish to read them on a larger screen, you can email them to yourself by tapping the 'Send by Email' button.

Fig 8, T&Cs **You must agree to these**

18 **All about iCloud** After 30 seconds or so, you will have the opportunity to set up one of the most revolutionary services Apple has created: iCloud – a fantastic cloud service that enable you to wirelessly keep your contacts, emails and calendars across multiple devices without you having to do anything. Tap 'What is iCloud' (Fig 9) to find out more about how it can benefit your life.

An Apple ID enables you to buy music, movies and books straight from the comfort of your iPad

Fig 9, iCloud **There to make your life easier**

Set up your iPad

Fig 10, Find My iPad **Locate a lost device**

Fig 11, Set up complete! **Start using your iPad**

Fig 12, Start using your iPad **Have fun!**

19 **Enable or disable iCloud** Tap the top option to enable iCloud – it's free (although there is the option to pay to increase your storage space, which you can do in Settings). If you choose not to enable it, you will miss the opportunity to set up Find My iPad in the next step of the process. You can, however, enable it from the Settings app once you've completed the activation.

20 **The Find My iPad service** If you misplace your iPad then Find My iPad will help you locate it on a map, play a sound or display a message. You can activate this service to sync the location of your device with your iCloud (Fig 10). If you lose your iPad then you can access the service from an iPhone, iPod touch or computer by visiting **www.icloud.com**.

21 **Diagnostics and Usage** The next screen deals with diagnostics and usage data. Basically, Apple likes to keep track of how its products are performing, so this screen allows you to send diagnostic data straight to Apple. If you wish to keep your information private, opt for 'Don't Send'. You can change your answer after activation from the Settings app, in the 'About' tab.

22 **Your last chance to restart** The diagnostics screen offers you once last chance to restart the activation process if you're not happy with the choices you've made. To restart the process, tap the Home button (the circular button at the bottom of the iPad) once, and a menu should pop up. You will then find the option to restart the activation, where you can make the choices you want.

23 **Set up is complete!** Congratulations! You have now worked your way through the entire set-up process. A screen will confirm that the process is complete (Fig 11), so what are you waiting for? Tap on the 'Start Using iPad' button to start using your iPad! If you press the Home button now to restart the procedure, you will just be taken to the Home Screen instead.

24 **Start using your iPad** You'll be presented with your Home Screen (Fig 12), so start tapping on icons to launch apps and find your way around and experiment with the gestures needed to operate your new device. Tap the Settings app and you'll have access to countless options, including ones that can reset the choices you made during the activation process.

You can change most of the choices you made during activation in the Settings app

The iPad Home Screen

Wi-Fi
This icon shows that you're connected to a network. See the icons below for more info

Time
You can change the format of the iPad's clock in the Settings app

Battery
This little icon will tell you how much battery power you have left

The apps
The heart and soul of the iPad. Tap on an icon to launch the app

The dock
Many people choose to place to their most used apps here in the Dock

Wallpaper
Your iPad's background is called the wallpaper. You can change it from the Settings app

Common iPad icons

 Wi-Fi
This icon shows that your iPad is successfully connected to the internet via a Wi-Fi network

 Lock
This tells you that your iPad is locked. Slide your finger across the bottom of the screen to unlock it

 Screen orientation lock
If you've set your iPad to stop switching from landscape to portrait, then you'll see this icon

 3G
If you see this icon then you're connected to the web over a 3G network. Not all iPads have this

 Do Not Disturb
If your iPad is set to Do Not Disturb mode then this icon will appear in the top-middle of the screen

 Alarm
Set an Alarm in the Clock app and this icon will appear in the top right, telling you that your Alarm is active

 4G
If you have a newer iPad, you may have access to the internet over 4G; in which case, this icon will be displayed

 Battery
The icon in the top-right shows you how much power you have left. A lightning bolt will show it's charging

 Location Services
The Location Services icon will appear to tell you that your iPad is determining your current location

 Airplane mode
If you put your iPad in Airplane mode then you can't access the internet or Bluetooth. Look for this icon

 Activity
The Activity icon will show up when something is happening on your iPad. Continue using it as normal

 Bluetooth
If you're paired with another device via Bluetooth, then this icon will show in the top-right-corner of the screen

Fig 1, Tap You will need to tap to launch apps

Hand gestures on your iPad

Learn the many ways you can control your iPad using the power of your fingers

1 Tap Tapping is the main way you will navigate your iPad. To open an app, you must tap it from your Home Screen, for example (Fig 1). You'll mainly be tapping the iPad to select things like web links in Safari, songs in Music, or pictures in Photos. You'll also need to tap to type on the on-screen keyboard when it appears in numerous apps such as Mail, Messages, Reminders and Notes.

Fig 2, Scroll Drag your finger to navigate around

2 Scroll Scrolling is when you drag your finger up or down the iPad's screen (Fig 2). This is most useful when the iPad can't fit all the information on one screen, so you need to slide your finger up to move the screen down and vice versa. This is most common in apps like Safari, Notes and, depending on the size of your collections, Music & Videos.

Fig 3, Swipe Use this gesture to switch pages

3 Swipe Where scrolling is vertical, swiping is horizontal – you just need to move your finger from left to right or vice versa. Once you start filling your iPad up with apps, you'll need to swipe to switch between pages of apps on the Home Screen (Fig 3). It's also needed to flick through the pages of your ebooks in iBooks and your magazines in Newsstand.

Fig 4, Drag Keep your finger held down

4 Drag Dragging is when you tap and hold your finger on the iPad, then drag it anywhere else on the screen. It's essential when moving apps around on the Home Screen. Tap and hold on an app until all other apps start wobbling. You can now drag it to its rightful place on the Home Screen. It's rarely used in other native apps, but common in third-party games.

5 Pinch Widely used among built-in and third-party apps, the pinch is a very useful gesture. To perform it, place two fingers on the screen and bring them together (Fig 5). It won't do anything on the Home Screen, but in many apps, including Photos and Maps, it zooms out the display. The more distance between your two fingers, the larger the zoom.

6 Spread The spread is essentially the opposite to the pinch: rather than bringing two digits together, you spread them apart (Fig 6). The effect is also the opposite, as rather than zooming out, you zoom in instead. This is particularly useful in Safari, when perhaps you need to zoom in read particularly small text; or Photos, when you want to inspect an image close-up.

Fig 5, Pinch Use this gesture to zoom out

Enable multitasking gestures by going to Settings, then General, and tapping the slider

Fig 6, Spread Use this gesture to zoom in

7 Five-finger pinch After enabling Multitasking Gestures in the General section of Settings, you will be able to perform a four or five-finger pinch. This works in most apps, and it will automatically take you back to the Home Screen. To perform the pinch, place all five fingers on the iPad screen and then bring them all towards a single point (Fig 7).

8 Five-finger scroll To access your recently used apps quickly, place all five fingers on the iPad screen and then move them all upwards (Fig 8). This will reveal the multitasking bar. From here you can choose a recently used app to use by tapping on it. If you tap and hold the app your will be able to remove it from the multitasking bar by tapping the red icon.

Fig 7, Five-finger pinch Use this to go Home

9 Five-finger swipe left/right To switch between apps quickly, place all your fingers on the iPad, then move from right to left (Fig 9). This gesture enables you to switch quickly between your current app and last used app without bringing up the multitasking bar. You don't get a selection of apps to choose from, so it's most useful when frequently moving between two apps.

Fig 8, Five-finger scroll up Access multitasking

10 Three-finger double-tap To enable these next three gestures, you must activate them by going into the Settings app, tapping on Accessibility and then choosing Zoom. Once enabled, if you double-tap the screen with three fingers you will zoom into the screen (Fig 10), similar to the Spread gesture. However, this gesture can be done anywhere – including the Home Screen.

11 Three-finger scroll When you're zoomed in with a three-finger double-tap, you can navigate around the screen by tapping and holding three fingers on the iPad and scrolling with them. This enables you to navigate around a zoomed app (or the Home Screen) while still letting you use normal gestures (such as Tap and Swipe) to operate the app.

Fig 9, Five-finger swipe Use this to switch apps

12 Three-finger drag The regular three-finger double-tap zoom is binary: it's either zoomed or it's not. To change the level of zoom, double-tap the iPad with three fingers again, but hold your fingers down after the second tap. Now scroll up or down to change the level of zoom. No matter how far you zoom in, a three-finger double-tap will bring you back to where you were.

Fig 10, Three-finger double-tap Enable it first

How to use your iPad

Learn how you can navigate and control your tablet with just a few buttons

Using an iPad is all about touch. There are very few hardware buttons included aside from the Home button on the front, the On/Off button at the top and the volume and mute keys on the side – so it's amazing that the iPad is capable of doing so much. As well as the basic tasks that you would expect it do – turn on and off, go on standby, etc – you can use its incredible multi-touch screen in combination with the buttons to multitask and arrange and manage your apps to your heart's content. Here are some of the basic actions you need to know about when navigating your iPad or iPad mini.

Turn your iPad off and on

2 Turn off Hold the On/Off button for a few seconds when the iPad's on.

1 The power button Hold down the On/Off button (at the top of the iPad) for a couple of seconds to turn the iPad on from a cold start. The 'Slide to Unlock' screen will appear quite quickly.

3 Slide to turn off Slide the red slider at the top to turn your iPad off.

Put your iPad to sleep

1 Don't hold it Press the On/Off button as normal, but do not hold it down for too long.

2 Standby mode The screen will go blank and the iPad is now in standby mode ready to start again.

Charging your iPad

1 **Use the kit** Plug the charger cable into the bottom of the iPad.

2 **Plug it** Plug the cable into the AC adaptor that comes with the iPad.

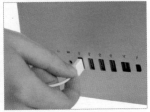

3 **USB** You can charge the iPad by USB, but it's not the quickest.

Multitasking

2 Select apps Slide your finger along the strip and tap on an app to load it.

1 Double-tap Home No matter what app you are in or where you are, double-tap the Home button to bring up the multitasking strip at the bottom of the screen. You should see more icons.

3 Close it Tap and hold on an app, then tap it again to close it down.

Manage your apps

2 Tap and drag Tap and hold on an app and drag it around to move it.

1 The Home Screen To navigate the Home Screen you will mostly use the swipe gesture to switch between multiple screens of icons. Simply swipe to the left to see the next screen and the right to return to the first.

3 Folders Drag one app over another to create an app folder.

Change the volume with headphones

1 Small buttons When the headphones are attached to the iPad, press the volume keys on the headphone cable.

2 Visual notifications You will see the volume level move on the screen as you press the buttons.

Change the volume

2 Via Multitasking Double-tap the Home button then swipe right.

1 The standard way In any app or in the Home Screen, you can simply press the volume key up or down to adjust the volume to your preference. This is the quickest way to adjust the sound levels.

3 Volume bar Now you can move the bar to your preferred volume.

Mute your iPad

1 The Mute button Slide the small button above the volume keys until you see a red marker. This will mute the iPad immediately, which is useful if you need to quickly stop any alerts or unwanted sounds from being heard.

Set the rotation lock

1 Use the strip Double-tap the Home button, slide the strip to the right and press the icon on the left.

2 The Mute button In Settings> General you can set the Side Switch to lock the rotation.

3 Landscape as well You can lock the rotation in both portrait and landscape modes.

2 Use the keys Hold the volume down button to mute.

3 Multitasking In the multitasking bar, move the slider all the way left.

Set the brightness

1 Use slider Double-tap the Home key and swipe the strip to the right. Notice the left slider.

2 Slide for brightness Move the slider left and right to adjust the brightness down and up.

Fig 1, Settings **Personalise your iPad**

Fig 2, App Store **Home to over 750,000 apps**

Fig 3, iTunes **Your online entertainment store**

Fig 4, Music **It's easy to listen to tunes in Music**

Fig 5, Safari **Browsing with tabs in Safari**

Applications

Your at-a-glance guide to what Apple's built-in iPad apps and App Store products can do for you

 Settings This is where you'll be able to change how your iPad works. You can connect to Wi-Fi, passcode-protect your device, and update the software, among many other things – all from this app. See page 32.

 App Store Although the built-in apps on your iPad are fantastic and will benefit your life in many different ways, you can download and buy more apps from Apple's built-in App Store. See page 40.

 iTunes Through this service you can download the hottest new albums and films, all from the comfort of your sofa. Just search for what you want, tap to buy and you'll have it in minutes. See page 46.

 Music Through this app you can listen to all of your purchased iTunes music, or music that you've transferred to your iPad. You can also set up playlists, rate your music collection and more. See page 52.

 Videos All of the TV shows and movies that you've downloaded from iTunes, along with any that you've transferred from your computer, will be viewable through this simple but effective app. See page 56.

 Safari This app is the best way to browse the internet on your iPad. Provided you're connected to Wi-Fi, you can use Safari to surf the web with tabs, browse privately or add items to read offline. See page 60.

 Mail Round-the-clock access to your email account is vital in today's world. The iPad Mail app helps you achieve this with an easy setup process and an intuitive interface. See page 66.

 Calendar If you need to organise your life, then check out the this app. It enables you to set up events, schedule appointments and basically take control of your day, week, month or even year! See page 70.

 Contacts Keep in touch with everyone with the iPad's built-in address book. If you can't find the Contacts app on the Home Screen, check the Utilities folder and it will likely be hiding in there. See page 74.

 Messages Although your iPad can't send text messages like an iPhone, it can take advantage of iMessage – a free messaging service that enables you to text users with other iOS devices. See page 78.

 Reminders If you find yourself regularly forgetting to do various tasks, use the Reminders app to give you a nudge. Set priorities and the exact times at which you need to be reminded. See page 82.

Fig 6, Mail Organise your emails with ease

 Notes Whether you need to jot down something important or just a whimsical thought, the easy-to-use Notes has you covered. All of your notes can also be synced to iCloud. See page 84.

 Maps This app will help you keep track of where you are in the world. It'll give you directions and show you how bad the traffic situation is, among many other things. See page 86.

 FaceTime Of course your iPad can't make a phone call, but it doesn't need to – it has FaceTime! Chat face-to-face with someone on another iOS device for free using a Wi-Fi connection. See page 96.

Fig 7, Reminders Never forget anything again

 Camera It may surprise you, but your iPad is capable of taking some very good pictures – especially the newer models. So use the exceptional built-in Camera app to your advantage. See page 98.

 Photos Once you've taken your photos or videos, you'll need a place to view them. Luckily, the Photos app is the perfect place for you to marvel at your images, and even make edits to them. See page 102.

 Game Center Take advantage of the millions of games available on iPad with Game Center. The app tracks your achievements and has leaderboards for many of the top games on iPad. See page 108.

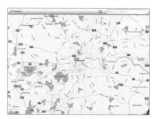

Fig 8, Maps Use Maps to find your way

 Newsstand The iPad has revolutionised digital media and its built-in Newsstand app is the best way to the consume it. Read digital magazines and newspapers with ease. See page 112.

 iBooks If you fancy reading some a bit more traditional on your iPad, then check out iBooks and the iBookstore. Here there are thousands of ebooks, which can all be read the way you want. See page 116.

 Pages This app turns your iPad into an amazing mobile word processor. You can create documents on the go in style by downloading Pages   · from the App Store. See page 120.

Fig 9, Photos Your virtual photo album

 Numbers This is an intuitive app, made by Apple and available from the App Store, that helps you create spreadsheets and present your data in a format that's easy to understand. See page 124.

 GarageBand By downloading this easy-to-master music-making app from the App Store, you can create multi-layered masterpieces with very little music knowledge. See page 132.

 iMovie If you want to turn your iPad movies into something special, then look no further. You can cut trailers, add special effects, and turn your family into the stars of professional-looking films. See page 136.

 iPhoto While the Photos app enables you to make rudimentary edits to your images, iPhoto is packed full of effects, brushes and swatches to make your photos stand out from the pack. See page 140.

Fig 10, Game Center Challenge your friends

Settings

We provide you with a guided tour around the nerve centre of your iPad

You'll use it to…

Connect to the internet
Establish a Wi-Fi connection to your device

Manage notifications
Determine how your iPad alerts you to various things

Personalise your iPad
Change the wallpaper, accessibility of your device and much more

Manage your iCloud
Connect to your cloud, and manage your storage and backup

Enable restrictions
Passcode-protect your device and set age restrictions on apps

Get social
Log into your Twitter and Facebook accounts to integrate them into your apps

Take control of your iPad

The Settings app, which you can launch by tapping its icon on the Home screen, is where you can tailor the functionality of your iPad to suit your needs, as well as personalise its appearance and services. In Settings, the categories are laid out in the left-hand column, freeing up the right-hand side to display the options (Fig 1).

Notification Center

Your iPad is constantly alerting you to new things – incoming emails, messages, Game Center friend requests and other assorted app alerts – and Notification Center lets you keep track of them easily by accessing a handy drop-down panel. To access your Notification Center, you swipe down from the top of the screen and all of your recent notifications will be displayed in a list. To tailor your Notification Center to your own specific needs, launch the Settings app and then tap on the Notifications section from the main

Fig 1 (above) In the Settings app, the functions are listed on the left and the options on the right

Fig 2 (right) Tap 'Edit' in your Notifications settings and press and hold on the list icon next to an app to change the order

Settings list. The main screen presents a list of apps that are in your Notification Center (and a list of those that are not, which you can add to the list). By tapping the Edit button in the top-right corner you can move apps between lists and change the order of how the apps appear in your Notification Center (Fig 2). To determine how your iPad receives alerts, tap on an app in the list and you can set the style of alert (how and where it will appear) and also whether or not it will flash up on your Lock screen.

iCloud

Apple's iCloud service is free to use and stores your music, photos, documents and more, and wirelessly sends them to all of your iOS devices (and Macs running OS X Mountain Lion or better) without you having to manually transfer files. Many of the built-in iPad apps, such as Contacts, Calendars and Reminders, use iCloud in some form to sync data across devices. You can determine which apps use iCloud by launching your Settings app and tapping iCloud. Move the sliders of the apps you wish to benefit from iCloud to the On position.

Manage your iCloud storage

Your iCloud account comes with five gigabytes of free storage as standard. To check how much space you have, tap on the Storage & Backup option in the iCloud section of Settings. To see how much of your free storage your apps use, tap on the Manage Storage option. You can delete data by tapping on an app and selecting the Edit button in the top-right corner. If you wish to buy more storage space for your iCloud, tap on the Buy More Storage option and then choose a capacity and price plan that suits you from the list.

You can view your personal iCloud account information by tapping on the account name

1 Go to Wi-Fi Settings
In Settings, tap on Wi-Fi and ensure that the slider is turned on.

2 Choose network
Your device will scan for networks. Tap on a Wi-Fi network to select it.

3 Enter password
You'll be prompted to enter your password. Do so, then tap 'Join'.

4 Connected
A tick will indicate that you are connected to your network.

Settings

Wirelessly update your iPad

Before October 2011, you had to connect your iPad to a computer and then use the iTunes app to update your system's software. Now times have changed and a computer is no longer required. You can activate and set up your iPad completely wirelessly and download free software updates on your device – as long as you have a Wi-Fi connection (see page 33 for how to connect your iPad to the internet). If you don't, you'll still have to connect to iTunes.

Fig 3 Tap on the Software Update option in the General section of Settings to see if your iPad needs updating

If your iPad's operating system (iOS) is out of date and there is a new, free update available then you will be notified via a small red alert that appears next to your Settings app icon. When this occurs, launch your Settings app and then tap on the General section in the settings list. At the top of this page will be an option called Software

Software update
The '1' in the General section means you have a Software Update available. Tap 'General' then 'Software Update'

Your iCloud account
Your iCloud account is tied in with your iTunes account that you have set up on your device to purchase media and apps

Available storage
Tap on the Storage & Backup option to review how much of your cloud you are using and buy more space, if necessary

Compatible apps
All of the apps that incorporate iCloud will be presented in a list. Move the sliders to the On position to activate their respective iCloud features

You can back up your iPad to iCloud straight away by tapping on the 'Back Up Now' option

Update (Fig 3) – tap on this and your device will start scanning for new updates, provided it is connected to a Wi-Fi network. If a new update is detected then you can opt to download and install it on your device. Be warned though that this may take a few minutes and your device will restart when the process is complete.

Back up your iPad

As you will have all sorts of important stuff on your iPad, iCloud will provide peace of mind by automatically backing up your device daily over Wi-Fi when your device is connected to a power source. Once you plug it in, everything is backed up without you having to lift a finger. When you set up a new iPad or need to restore the information on one you already have, iCloud does all the heavy lifting for you. Just connect your device to Wi-Fi, enter your Apple ID (which you created when you activated your iPad), and then all your purchased music, TV shows, books and apps, will appear on your device. To activate this service, launch your Settings app and tap on the iCloud section. Next, tap on the Storage & Backup option and ensure iCloud Backup is turned on. All of your data will be backed up when your iPad is plugged in, locked and connected to Wi-Fi.

How to back up your iPad

1 Go to iCloud Settings
Tap on the Storage & Backup option and turn on the iCloud Backup option.

2 Initiate back up
Ensure that your iPad is plugged in, locked and connected to Wi-Fi.

Set keyboard shortcuts

1 Access keyboard settings
In the Settings app, tap on General and then Keyboard.

2 Enable shortcuts
Move the shortcut sliders to 'On' to enable the various features.

3 Adding shortcuts
Tap on Add New Shortcut to start adding your own.

4 Creating shortcuts
Type in a word or phrase followed by the shortcut you wish to use.

Settings

Set a passcode

1 Tap Passcode Lock
In the General section in Settings, tap on the Passcode Lock options.

2 Turn it on
Tap on the Turn Passcode On option at the top of the page.

3 Enter a code
Enter and confirm a four-digit code to protect your device.

4 Secure passcode
Turn off Simple Passcode to use your full keyboard for a code.

To prevent other users buying apps, change the Require Password option to 'Immediately'

Change the Wallpaper

If you want to change the appearance of your iPad then you can do so under the Brightness and Wallpaper settings. When you tap on this option you will see the brightness options at the top – which basically consists of a slider to adjust the brightness and an option to activate Auto-Brightness.

To change the wallpaper, tap on the Wallpaper options and you will be presented with two sections to tap on. The first, called Wallpaper, allows you to choose from a selection of pre-loaded wallpapers that are already installed on your device and the second, called Saved Photos, lets you fashion a background out of a photograph in your Photos app. Whichever option you choose, tap on your selection and it will be displayed full-screen. Now simply tap either the Set Lock Screen or Set Home Screen buttons to instantly set the image as your chosen backdrop on either your Lock Screen or your Home Screen. Alternatively, tap on the Set Both option to use the same image for both screens.

There are many apps available from the App Store that provide hundreds of great additional wallpapers for your device. These can be downloaded to your Photos app and then used from there.

Impose restrictions

1 Tap on Restrictions
In the General Settings page, tap on the Restrictions section.

2 Enable restrictions
Tap on Enable Restrictions and then set a four-digit passcode.

Enable parental restrictions

As you have invested quite a significant sum of money in your iPad, as well as the various apps and iTunes media content that you have bought, then you will naturally want to impose restrictions on who can access your material. Likewise, if your device is shared throughout the family then enabling restrictions will mean that inappropriate material cannot be accessed through the device and expensive apps can't be purchased by accident.

To start enabling restrictions, go to the General Settings section and then tap on Restrictions. By tapping on the Enable Restrictions option at the top of the page, you will first be required to enter a four-digit passcode. Do so and then move the sliders to the On position of the apps that may be accessed and then review the list of allowed content. To impose greater restrictions, go back to the General page and tap on Passcode Lock (Fig 4).

Fig 4 To impose greater restrictions and gain more control over what your kids can do, turn on the Passcode Lock function

Restrictions
If your device is used regularly by others, then you can set certain restrictions to protect your device, and them, from tapping on the wrong thing

Passcode Lock
Activate this feature to protect your device from unwanted users. You can set a four-digit code or something more complicated

Lock rotation
Sick of your iPad screen flipping between portrait and landscape when you accidentally tilt your device? Then lock it here

Keyboard
You can set the keyboard up to be both easier to use and quicker to type by adjusting the various Keyboard settings

Change Wallpaper

To access the Spotlight search, swipe with one finger from left to right on the Home screen

1 Find your options
Launch Settings and then tap on Brightness & Wallpaper.

Customise and access Spotlight

As if finding things on your iPad wasn't simple enough, the built-in Spotlight Search function lets you type criteria into a search field and then unearth it instantly. To use this feature, simply swipe right from your device's primary Home Screen and then the screen will dim, a small search field will appear and your iPad's keyboard will pop up to allow you to enter keywords into the search field. The results will appear below.

2 Tap on Wallpaper
Tap on the Lock or Home screen image in the Wallpaper area.

In Settings, you can determine what is searched for and the order in which the results appear. To check this out for yourself, go to the General section in Settings and you should see a category called 'Spotlight Search'. Tap on this. The screen that you are taken to is little more than a list of search categories that relate to content on your device. You can activate or deactivate content to search for in this list and the order of the items reflects the order in which the search results will be displayed.

To change the order in which the search results are displayed, press and hold on the list icon next to each category and then drag it up or down into a new position and then release so that it snaps into place – that's all there is to it.

3 Pick a background
You can use an existing wallpaper or one of your own photos.

How to start Picture Frame

4 Set wallpaper
Select one and choose either Set Lock Screen or Set Home Screen.

1 Tap the picture
On your iPad's Lock screen, tap on the picture frame icon next to the slider.

2 Enjoy the show
Picture Frame mode will instantly kick in, so sit back and enjoy.

Turn your iPad into a picture frame

One of the coolest features of the iPad is that you can turn it into a digital picture frame ornament to adorn any living space and display your images in stunning high definition. You can access this feature from your iPad's Lock screen – to the right of the slider used to unlock your device you will see a small picture frame icon, tap this to initiate the Picture Frame feature.

The Picture Frame feature will then present a digital slideshow of all of the photos on your device and you can tailor the options in your Settings app. In the list of settings, you will see Picture Frame listed between Brightness & Wallpaper and Privacy, tap on it and you will see various options that you can change – such as the transition effect between images, the duration each photo is displayed for and more.

Fig 5 The Picture Frame feature has its own options page in Settings

Do Not Disturb
Since iOS 6, you have been able to make sure you receive no notifications by moving the Do Not Disturb slider to On

Transitions
Choose one of the transitions to determine how your photos will transition into each other - Origami is a bit more creative

Length of time
Here you can choose how long each photo is shown for – you can choose to display images for 2, 3, 5, 10 or 20 seconds

All photos or albums
Use this option to choose from specific album or all photos on your iPad, tapping 'Albums' will bring up the list of albums

App Store

Your gateway to a rich source of apps is via the intuitive App Store – a bustling marketplace that is always open for business

You'll use it to…

Discover apps
Clearly defined sections help you find and discover exciting new apps

Search for apps
If you know the name of an app, enter it in the search field and you'll find it in seconds

Purchase apps
Buy and download apps to your iPad

Gift apps
Send an app to someone special

Review apps
Give a little customer feedback

Get recommendations
Use the Genius feature to see what apps best suit you

Shop for apps

The App Store will be your most-used iPad app because it is here that you purchase and download content for your device (Fig 1). Thankfully, it is a very user-friendly environment where you can discover what's hot and make informed purchases in seconds.

Search the App Store

Considering that the shelves of the App Store have swelled to over 900,000 products, with 375,000 specifically for iPad, being able to find what you need quickly is of the ultimate importance – so it's just as well that there is an intuitive search engine on hand to help.

If you know the name of the app you're looking for then enter it into the Search field (Fig 2). As you type the letters, matches will instantly start being made with what you're typing. If you see what you want in the list of suggestions, then just tap on it to instantly go

Fig 1 (above) The storefront is brimming with attractive offers and sections

Fig 2 (right) Start typing keywords into the search engine to find what you want

to that page. If you're not sure of what you're looking for, then there are plenty of handy pointers to steer you in the right direction. The 'Featured' section is a good starting point as it showcases all of the latest eye-catching apps of significance. From there you can use the Top Charts and Categories tabs at the bottom of the screen to see what's currently popular or begin searching in an area of interest.

Browse the Top Charts

If you start browsing the App Store without a clue of what to look for or where to go to look for it, then help is at hand. Using the touch icons at the bottom of the screen, tap on the Top Charts section and you will be presented with a rundown of the most popular apps available on the store – both full price and free. You can use this as a barometer to see what's hot in the world of apps and see if any popular apps jump out at you.

Genius

Like with iTunes, in which the Genius feature can be utilised to get song recommendations based on the music in your library, the App Store boasts a similar feature. While in the App Store, tap the Genius button at the bottom of the window and you'll be taken to a screen full of Genius recommendations based on the apps that are currently installed on your iPad. The lay-out of this page is simple to digest as you can clearly see the app that inspired the recommendation, purchase the recommended app straight from the Genius page, or register that you are not interested by tapping the button underneath. If you then tap on the 'More' arrow then you can scroll through additional possibilities.

iPad App Collections groups some great apps together for you to browse and download

Redeem a gift card

1 Tap on Featured
Make sure that you're in the Featured section of the store.

2 Tap Redeem
Tap on the Redeem button at the bottom of the page.

3 Tap on Code
Tap on the Code field and then enter your code and hit Redeem.

4 Redeem your app
Sign in and your gifted app will subsequently download.

App Store

Fig 3 Tap on the price (or 'Free' if it's free) to purchase and download the app. You may have to enter your Apple ID

Purchase an app

Being the only source of gaining apps for your iPad, the App Store is, as you would expect, a quick and easy way to shop for new apps, and purchasing them really couldn't be simpler. You will already be logged into the App Store with your registered Apple ID, which should have your billing details attached.

If you haven't already added the details of a valid credit or debit card for your app funding then tap on the Featured page at the App Store, scroll down to the bottom and then tap on your Apple ID. Select 'View Apple ID' from the menu and then tap on the Payment Information option. You can now select a card type and enter all of the required information so that all app purchases will be made using that card. Now you can tap on the price of an app and

Featured apps
All the latest significant new additions to the App Store will be showcased in the main shop window under Featured

Store sections
You will be able to access specific stores for Top Charts, Featured, Genius recommendations and more by tapping these buttons

Buying apps
Tap on the price of a product to initiate the purchase and download process

Search
Enter keywords into the search field to help you find apps featured within the store

No reviews for the current version? Then look further back by tapping on the 'All Versions' button

then complete the purchase by inputting your Apple ID password (Fig 3). You will still need to enter your Apple ID password when downloading free apps, but you don't have to assign a credit or debit card to do so.

Review and rate apps

App feedback is good, not only because feedback – good or bad – gets back to the developer and lets them know how the public is receiving their apps and how they can make them better. It also provides information for your fellow iPad users to help them make informed decisions on whether to buy a particular app or not, so if you have the time and the inclination, then why not leave your own mini app review?

To do this, tap on an app (it has to be an app you own for you to be able to review it) to access its info page and then scroll down. You will see a section called Customer Ratings, with a row of stars underneath. Tap on the stars to rate the app out of five – as you tap them they will be coloured in gold. You can also write your own review for the product by tapping on the Write a Review link that is situated under the Customer Reviews. A box will then appear with

Submit a review of an app

1 Tap to rate
Tap on the row of stars to rate an app that you own out of five.

2 Write review
Tap on the Write a Review link and then submit your thoughts.

Recommend an app

1 Tap on The Share button
Go to an app's info page and tap the Share button (a box and arrow).

2 Email
If you tap Mail, then you can send an email with the app's info.

3 Message
Tapping Message enables you to send an iMessage (see page 78).

4 Tweet
If you have a Twitter account set up, you can also tweet about it.

Re-download an app

1 Go to Purchased
Tap Purchased at the bottom of the App Store screen.

2 Tap Not On This iPad
Now tap on the Not On This iPad tab at the top of the page.

3 Tap cloud icon
iCloud icons will be visible beside your previous purchases. Tap one.

4 Sign in and download
Enter your Apple ID password and the app will start downloading.

To rename a folder, tap the 'X' at the end of the title bar and then rename it whatever you want

spaces for a review title and your text. Once done, hit Submit to get your review published on the page.

Update your apps

Apps are constantly evolving, improving and updating, but rather than charge you for an app, get customer feedback and then charge you again when an update comes out, the updates are always completely free once you have bought the product. What's more, you don't have to trawl the App Store to see if your favourite apps have updates because there's a section dedicated to them, which is accessible through the aptly named Updates tab at the bottom of the interface. If you have any updates ready, you'll see a red bubble with the number of apps that need updating inside it.

Tap on this and all of the apps that you have installed on your device that have been updated will be listed. You can then scroll down the list and tap the Update button next to a particular app to update it. Alternatively, you can tap on the Update All button in the top-left corner of the screen to automatically download all applicable updates in one fell swoop.

Create a folder of apps

1 Press and hold
Press down on an app icon until they all start jiggling.

2 Stack them
Drag the icon on top of another icon and then release.

Manage your apps

Whenever you purchase an app it will be downloaded to your device and appear in an available slot on one of your Home screens. However, the position it takes up upon download isn't set in stone and you can move your apps around freely and place them wherever you want – even creating new folders to store them all in.

    To move apps around, press and hold on an app icon until they all start to shake (and an 'X' appears next to each icon that you can press to delete the app) then press and hold on the icon and move it to a new position. If you want to move the app to a different Home Screen, drag it to the side of the screen and, within a second, the next or previous Home Screen will appear, depending on the side of the screen you move the app to (Fig 4). Place the app where you want it to sit and then release. To create folders for apps, simply drag one app icon onto another and a folder will form.

Fig 4 Drag an app icon to the sides to move it to a different screen

Update All
To get all available updates, tap on the Update All button in the top-left corner

Updates tab
A red bubble on the Updates tab tells you that you have apps that need updating

Manual update
Tap on the Update button next to a listed app in order to manually update it

Update info
The details of what each update contains will appear alongside the name of the app

iTunes

Let your iPad entertain you with music, movies and TV shows – all of which can be bought right here

You'll use it to…

Browse for items
Sections make it easy to find new content and great deals

Purchase media
Buying new music and movies is easy

Discover new media
Search and roam for interesting items

Gift items
Buy and send a gift to a loved one

Make use of Genius
Get artist recommendations and create smart playlists

Get an education
Get access to a wealth of study materials with the iTunes U app

Buy music and movies

Although there are links to the respective sections of the iTunes Store within the Music and Videos apps, you can access the store direct from its own app on the Home screen and browse for content at your leisure. And there is plenty to explore (Fig 1).

The Categories in iTunes

Navigating your way around the iTunes Store is made easy by a series of tabs at the bottom of the screen that allow you to breeze freely to the various store categories that include Music, Films, TV Programmes, Audiobooks and more (Fig 2). Tap on a category to access a front-page relating to that particular category that is packed full of featured offers and attractions.

If you have bought things previously from the iTunes Store on other iOS devices (like iPhone or iPod touch) then, thanks to Apple's iCloud service, you will be able to re-download them again onto

Fig 1 (above) The iTunes Store is a thriving hive of digital entertainment

Fig 2 (right) Use the tabs at the bottom of the interface to jump straight to the various store categories

your iPad – just tap on the Purchased category, then on the 'Not on this iPad' tab at the top of the page and then choose a song and tap on the cloud icon. If you are currently downloading content from the iTunes Store then you will be able to track the progress of your purchases by tapping on the Downloads category.

Search for and sample a song

One of the good things about the iTunes Store is that it allows you to try before you buy. First of all, search for an album or artist you may be interested in by tapping the search field in the top corner of the screen. Now tap on an album and then tap on a track name to listen to a sizeable chunk to determine if it is what you're looking for. You can end the preview at any time by either tapping on another song or tapping the Stop button in the middle of the playback wheel.

Download songs

Purchasing and downloading songs from the iTunes Store is a quick and easy process that can be done in seconds. We have already explored how you can search for songs and preview tracks, and if you decide that you would like to go ahead with the purchase then tap on the price and it will turn into a green 'Buy Song' button.

If you then wish to go ahead with the purchase, you will be prompted to enter your Apple ID password before the track will start downloading – this is a security measure to ensure that you don't buy items by tapping on them accidentally. You can track the progress of this by tapping on the Downloads category at the bottom of the screen.

If you are lucky enough to be gifted a redeem code, scroll down the Music page and tap Redeem

Download a TV series

1 iTunes
First, head to the iTunes app to browse the available shows.

2 TV
Tap TV at the bottom and you will be taken to the TV show section.

3 Select a show
Pick a show and it will bring up the information for your selection.

4 Buy the series
Tap the price to buy the series, or check the ratings and reviews first.

iTunes

Fig 3 The iTunes U app is downloadable from the App Store

Introducing iTunes U

If you are currently studying at school or higher education then the iTunes Store also provides a wealth of materials to help make learning easier. This service, called iTunes U, was available as a store category, accessible via one of the tabs at the bottom of the screen in iOS 5. Since the release of iOS 6, though, it has migrated out of the iTunes app into its own standalone app that operates exactly like Music, Videos, iBooks and Newsstand, allowing you to jump straight to the applicable section of the iTunes Store (Fig 3).

The iTunes U part of the store is laid out like the other sections, with its own Featured, Top Charts and Categories sections, and you can also use the search bar to find what you want. Once you have found a set of study materials that you are interested in, tap on the

Store sections
You will be able to access specific stores for Music, Films, TV Programmes, Audiobooks and more at the bottom of the screen

Featured sections
All of the latest significant new additions to the iTunes Store will be showcased in the main shop window and heavily flagged

Buying
Tap on the price of a product to start the purchase and download process. Ensure you are logged in and have funding set up

Search the store
Enter keywords into the search field to find specific artists, songs, movies or programmes featured within the store

It will cost £21.99 a year to use iTunes Match, so consider how much use you will get out of it

title to open the info page and then hit the Subscribe button. The materials will then be downloaded and populate the shelves of your iTunes U app, where you can access and browse them at your leisure whenever you are ready to start studying.

iTunes Match

Since iTunes works in perfect harmony with Apple's iCloud service, any music that you purchase, regardless of which device you're using to make the purchase, will be automatically pushed to your other iOS 6 or better devices.

iTunes Match (which requires an annual subscription) is an extension of this service which matches the music on your computer, that has been imported from CDs, to its digital iTunes Store counterpart, and stores it all in your iCloud ready for use. iTunes determines which songs in your collection are available in the iTunes Store and any music with a match is automatically added to iCloud for you to listen to at any time, on any device. Since there are more than 20 million songs in the iTunes Store, chances are your music is already in iCloud.

Enabling iTunes Match

1 Subscribe
On your computer, launch iTunes, click iTunes Match and subscribe.

2 Go to Settings
On your iPad, go to the Music Settings and enable iTunes Match.

Pause a download

1 Download content
Start downloading content, such as a song or audiobook.

2 Go to Downloads
A number appears next to the Downloads tab. Tap on it.

3 Tap to pause
Tap on the pause button to halt the download process.

4 Resume download
When you are ready to resume downloading, tap the arrow.

Subscribe to podcasts

1 Tap on Podcasts
Tap on the Podcasts section down at the bottom of the app.

2 Check the Top Charts
You will be taken to the Featured section. Tap on Top Charts.

3 Find a podcast
Browse what's popular or search for something and then select it.

4 Subscribe and download
Subscribe or download episodes, then play them in the Music app.

When you buy alert tones they will be added to the Sounds section in General Settings

iTunes in the Cloud

With iCloud, the music that you purchase in iTunes appears automatically on all of your mobile iOS devices and Macs running OS X Mountain Lion. You can also download your past iTunes purchases where you want, when you want (Fig 4). iCloud can automatically download new music purchases to all your devices over Wi-Fi – or over a cellular network if your iPad has that capability. Which means you can buy a song from iTunes on your iPad at home, and find it waiting for you on your iPhone during your morning commute, all without even having to sync.

Any music you have purchased in the past will also be easily accessible. Simply tap on the 'Purchased' tab and you will be able to view an alphabetical list of all of your past purchases. If one of the items isn't currently on your iPad then highlight it and then tap on the cloud icon that is next to the song name. The song will instantly start downloading to your device and will then be playable through the Music app.

You can also subscribe to iTunes Match, which will match songs in the iTunes catalogue with those ripped from CDs on your computer and allow you to access them any time you want.

Finding tones

1 The More menu
Tap the 'More' menu in the top bar, then select 'Tones'.

2 Purchase tones
Browse products and then purchase tones as you would other media.

The Tones Store

Since the release of iOS 5, iTunes now includes the Tones Store, which provides access to a variety of different ringtones and sound effects. However, unlike on iPhone, finding this section in your iPad iTunes app isn't easy and requires specific hunting using the search field. If you search for 'Tones' then the results will throw up suggestions from the Ringtones and Alert Tones sections of the store, so you can use this as stepping stones to search for more content. When searching for specific items using the smart search engine, the chances are that the app will throw up ringtones as suggestions so you can jump straight to that product from the search page. Purchasing tones is easy and uses exactly the same process as if you were buying music or film. Simply tap on a price next to a product to make the purchase and download the product.

Fig 4 Re-download past iTunes purchases on your current device for free

Preview tracks
Tap on a track name in order to listen to a preview of the song that you have chosen

Album info
Tap on an album to open its information page and view info such as release date, and so on

Artist pages
The iTunes store links a band's group of work together. Swipe through to see more albums

Buying songs
Tap on the price and then 'Buy Song' to purchase and download your selected tracks

Music

The Music app enables you to belt out the hits in style on your iPad

You'll use it to...

Play music
A simple set of controls let you belt out your tunes

Make playlists
Create new playlists on the fly quickly and easily

Buy tracks and albums
Access the iTunes Store to grab new songs

Use Genius
Allow the app to create playlists for you

Access podcasts
Play all of your downloaded podcasts

Searching content
Find what you want, when you want to listen to it

Listen to music on the go

Replacing what was the iPod app, Music is where you can listen to all of the top tunes that you have synced or purchased on your iPad. Through this app you can listen to tracks, create playlists and shop for new music through the iTunes store (Fig 1).

Import songs

There are numerous ways to import music to play on your iPad. The most direct route is by purchasing it straight from the iTunes store on your device, and you can do this by tapping on the Store button in the lower-left corner of the Music interface and then browsing the store. While in the iTunes store, you can also tap on the Purchased tab at the bottom of the interface and this will list all of the music that you have bought previously on other devices.

Thanks to the power of iCloud, all of your previous purchases are tracked, so tap on the 'Not on this iPad' tab at the top of the

Fig 1 (above) You can view your music by Songs, Artist or Album in the Music interface and even visit the iTunes store

Fig 2 (right) You can re-download past purchases that aren't on your iPad, as everything is tracked by iCloud

window, select a track and then tap the cloud icon to re-download it on your current device (Fig 2). Of course, you can also import songs by connecting your device to your computer and syncing through iTunes or, alternatively, opening iTunes on your computer, highlighting songs in your music library and then manually dragging them to your iPad in the left-hand column.

Playing your music

First and foremost, the Music app is there to enable you to play and listen to music on your iPad, and the controls for doing this are simple to get to grips with. Start off by choosing music to listen to by selecting a tab at the bottom of the screen and navigating to a song, then tap on it to start playing it. The controls in the top-left corner of the interface allow you to play/pause the current song and skip to the next or previous songs.

Add lyrics from iTunes

If you want to sing along to your favourite songs through the Music app then there is a way to get lyrics displayed on screen while the song is playing, but this involves using iTunes on your computer.

Start off by searching online for the song lyrics and then copy them by highlighting them and pressing Cmd (Mac) or Ctrl (Windows) plus C. Now open iTunes, right-click on the corresponding song and choose the 'Get Info' option from the menu. In the window that appears, click on the Lyrics tab and then paste the copied lyrics into the window (Cmd/Ctrl+V) and tap OK. You will now need to delete the original song off of your iPad and then re-sync it with iTunes to get the lyrics onto your iPad.

If viewing album art when playing songs, skip tracks by swiping left or right across the screen

Rate your albums

1 Start playing
Select an album from your library and then start playing it.

2 Tap art
Tap on the album art on the top bar, next to the playback controls.

3 Tap the list icon
Tap the art to shrink it then tap the list icon in the bottom corner.

4 Tap the dots
Tap the row of dots above the track listing to rate out of five.

Music

Fig 3 Access your Genius playlists by
tapping on the Playlists tab at the bottom
of the screen

Genius playlists

A Genius playlist is a collection of songs from your library that work well together and you can create Genius playlists in iTunes on your computer and sync them to your iPad or directly on the device itself. Genius has a knack of stringing similar songs together, creating smooth playlists by compiling tracks you perhaps never thought to place side by side in a running order – perfect for a party.

To use Genius on iPad, first turn on Genius in iTunes on your computer and then sync the iPad with iTunes. Genius mixes are synced automatically (unless you manually manage your music and decide which mixes you want to sync in iTunes). Back on the iPad, you can play the mixes by tapping on the Playlists tab at the

Playback controls
You can play/pause and skip songs using the simple set of controls in the top-left corner of the screen

Advanced controls
The top bar also features controls to repeat songs, shuffle songs, scrub through songs, use Ping and add the song to a Genius playlist

Volume control
You can pump up the volume by dragging this slider to the right position. Press and hold and move the slider

Section tabs
Tabs at the bottom of the interface allow you to find music by Song, Artist or Album, access playlists and (by tapping More) access your downloaded podcasts

You can scrub through songs by pressing on the line on the top bar and then dragging it

bottom of the Music app interface and selecting the Genius playlist (Fig 3). If you wish to refresh a Genius Playlist, open the playlist on your iPad and tap Refresh. If you want to make a new Genius playlist using a different song, simply tap the Genius atom icon on the top bar when the song is playing and a new playlist will be created.

Manage your playlists

Creating and managing playlists on your iPad is easy through the Music app. As well as creating new playlists from scratch, you can also edit playlists that have been synced across from iTunes in order to update them or make subtle tweaks here and there.

To create a new playlist, simply tap on the Playlists tab and then tap the New button in the top-right corner. Give your new playlist a name, tap Save and then start adding songs from your library by either tapping on the song itself or the '+' icon next to it. When you have finished adding, tap Done and your playlist will be complete. If you wish to edit an existing playlist, select it from the Playlists page and then tap the Edit button. You can now delete songs by tapping the '-' icon next to each song or change the order by holding on the list icon next to each song and dragging it up or down.

Create a playlist

1 Tap on New
On the Playlists screen, tap New, name your playlist and then tap Save.

2 Add songs
Add songs by tapping on a song name or the '+' icon.

Delete songs

1 Locate the song
Use the tabs at the bottom of the screen to locate the song.

2 Swipe left
Swipe left on a song and a Delete option will appear. Tap it.

3 Instant erase
The song will then be deleted without warning, so be sure.

4 Delete entire albums
Press and hold on an album and then tap on the 'X' icon.

Videos

The Videos app lets you watch movies and TV shows anywhere on your iPad

You'll use it to...

Watch videos
Watch films, music videos and TV shows on your iPad

Shop for content
Access the iTunes Store in-app to shop for videos

Stream to Apple TV
Beam your videos straight to the big screen

Stream videos from your computer
Watch your computer video library remotely on your iPad

Watch anywhere
Take your device with you and watch videos wherever you are

Manage your movies
Sync files from your computer and delete them once watched

Fig 1 (above) Viewing movies and TV shows on your device is simple through the Videos app

Watch TV shows and movies on iPad

You can use your iPad to watch movies, music videos and TV shows, transforming it into a mobile multiplex to view what you want, on demand. Using the Videos app is easy, so sit back, relax and enjoy the show (Fig 1).

Rent & buy from iTunes

Just like the Music app, Videos features a launch pad to the iTunes Store, in this case the visual entertainment section – where you can shop for films to rent or films to buy outright. Simply tap the Store button in the top-left corner of the main Videos interface to be warped to the iTunes Store and then use the search field to find what you want.

When you have found a film, tap on the View button next to the title and a box will appear that provides a plot synopsis, credits, details and user reviews (Fig 2). More importantly it also features a

Fig 2 (right) Tap a movie in iTunes and then choose to buy or rent it. Note that both options aren't always available

button that allows you to preview the movie through your Videos app and options to buy or rent the movie. If you're buying then the system is the same as purchasing music or apps – just tap 'Buy' and the film will download to your device.

Renting is slightly different – you still download it, but it will expire after a certain number of days and, once you start a movie, you have a limited amount of time to finish watching it. It does mean you will never have to pay a late fee though!

Import videos from your computer

If you don't want to buy directly from the iTunes Store through the app then you can also import videos from your computer via iTunes. Simply connect your device and then click on the Movies section under your Library to view all of the movies on your machine. Now you can either drag the film to your iPad, which is in the sidebar, or perform a sync instead to get your flicks onto your device.

Playing your videos

As with music, playing videos on your device is easy. From the main Videos app screen, use the tabs that are located at the top to choose to view Movies or Music Videos and then tap on a video that is displayed in your chosen section.

When the video is launched, a simple set of controls at the bottom of the screen allow you to play or pause the action, skip chapters and adjust the volume. You can also scrub through the action by swiping along the bar at the top of the screen and go full-screen by tapping the button in the top-right corner.

You can also adjust the viewing area size by double-tapping anywhere on the screen

Change scrub speed

1 Tap scrub bar
Press your finger down on the dot situated on the scrub bar.

2 Scrub rate
The scrub rate will be displayed (either high or half-speed).

3 Swipe down
Slide your finger down to change to the alternate speed.

4 Start scrubbing
You can now slide your finger along the bar at the selected rate.

Videos

Home Sharing

With Home Sharing, you can play movies and TV shows on your iPad from the iTunes library on your Mac or PC. To use this feature, both your iPad and your computer need to be on the same Wi-Fi network and, on your computer, you must have iTunes open and running. In iTunes, click on the Advanced menu and then turn on Home Sharing and ensure that both your computer and iPad are logged in and using the same Apple ID.

To ensure that you are logged into the same Apple ID on your iPad, go to Settings, tap on the Music or Videos sections and then log your details under the Home Sharing section. Once the system

Fig 3 You can access your Mac's movie library to watch on your iPad

End viewing
If you wish to stop watching, tap the Done button and resume where you left off later

Playback controls
Simple controls let you play and pause the action, skip backwards or forwards through chapters and adjust the volume

Rewind
Press and hold the dot on this bar, and by sliding it to the left you can rewind the action

Screen size
Tapping this button will make the video fill the screen. Tap it again to return to the original dimensions

With iPad 2 or later, you can mirror the screen on a TV wirelessly using AirPlay Mirroring and Apple TV

has been set up, a new tab will appear at the top of your Videos interface called Shared. Tap on this and then choose to access your computer's library (Fig 3). Now simply select something to watch, sit back and enjoy. To deactivate this service, click on the Advanced menu on your computer again and then turn off Home Sharing to instantly sever the connection.

AirPlay

If you have an Apple TV system in your home then you can stream video content from your iPad to your TV wirelessly using AirPlay. This is easy to set up and means that you can use your iPad to shop for movies to buy or rent and then use your device as a remote control to play them on your big TV screen.

To start streaming video with AirPlay, start playing a video on your iPad and then tap the AirPlay button. Next, choose your Apple TV from the list of AirPlay devices and then select it to start beaming the video across. If the AirPlay button doesn't appear or your Apple TV doesn't appear in the list, check to make sure that both devices are connected to the same wireless network. You can also stream videos using various cables, including AV cables and VGA Adapters.

Streaming videos with AirPlay

1 Start playback
Start watching a video, tap on the AirPlay icon, then tap Apple TV.

2 Nothing on iPad
While your video is playing on Apple TV, your iPad will display this screen.

Delete videos

1 Locate video
Find a video that you no longer want on your device.

2 Press and hold
Press down on the video until an 'X' appears in the corner.

3 Tap to delete
Tap on the 'X' icon and a message will appear asking if you're sure.

4 Instant removal
Tap Delete and then video will be deleted from your device.

Safari

Safari

The Safari app makes browsing the internet on your
iPad both quick and simple

You'll use it to...

Browse the web
Trawl your favourite sites on your iPad

Keep tabs
Keep your favourite pages open

Read clearly
Read stories in a clean, uncluttered Safari
Reader window

Save a Reading List
Save your favourite stories to read
whenever you want – even offline

Share web pages
Tweet or add pages to your Facebook status
on the fly

Add links
Create handy Home screen shortcuts for
your favourite web pages

Surf with ease

Browsing the internet on your iPad is a simple and intuitive
experience made easy by the touch-screen interface and simple
gestures that mean you can tap on links to access them, pinch and
expand your fingers to zoom and swipe your finger up or down to
scroll the pages. The portability of the iPad also means you can surf
the net anywhere you have a Wi-Fi connection (Fig 1).

Browse the web

To start browsing the web on your iPad, ensure that your device is
connected to a Wi-Fi network (which you can do in your Settings
app) and then launch Safari and tap on the address field or search
window. Use the pop-up keyboard to enter a URL or a search
keyword and then the page should load in the main window.

A simple interface makes it easy to bookmark your favourite
pages. To the left of the address bar is an share icon that you can

Fig 1 (above) Trawling the internet is
second nature on an iPad

Fig 2 (right) Tap the share button to access
a wide range of options

touch to bring up a list of options (Fig 2). We'll come to some of these later but the top option, 'Add Bookmark', provides all the options you need to store your favourite pages for easy access.

Once you have added a bookmark, you can rename it whatever you want. So rather than store it as the long, often convoluted web address, you can shorten it to something snappier. Tap on the Bookmarks option and you'll be able to store it in the Bookmarks Menu – accessible from this list – or save in the Bookmarks Bar, which sits along the top of the page under the address bar and provides quick and easy access to your favourite sites.

Browse with tabs

Tabbed web browsing allows users to keep up to nine web pages open simultaneously. These pages will be arranged as tabs at the top of the window with the first couple of words of each web site visible so that you can see what they are and access them easily by tapping the tab that corresponds to the site you wish to visit. Adding new tabs is easy. While on any web page, press the '+' icon to the far-right of the tabs to open a new window and instantly store the page you were on as a tab.

iCloud tabs

Using iCloud, browsing the internet on your iPad has never been easier – you can start browsing on one device and continue exactly where you left off on another.

With iCloud tabs, any tabs that you have open on your iPad will be viewable on any other device that is running iOS 6 or higher, like an iPhone or Mac (as long as it is running OS X Mountain Lion or better) and vice versa. All you have to do is tap the Bookmarks icon

Tap the open book icon and then History. You'll see a button here that lets you 'Clear History'

Enable iCloud Tabs

1 Activate iCloud
Log into the same iCloud account on all of your devices.

2 Open Safari
Open up the Safari app and load a new tab.

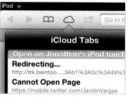

3 Choose iCloud tabs
Next to the address bar, tap the iCloud icon.

4 Tap on link
These are the open tabs on your other devices. Tap to access.

Safari

at the top of the screen, choose iCloud Tabs and any tabs that you have open on your other devices (which are connected to the same iCloud account) will be selectable.

Fig 3 The Reader option lets you view a cleaner version of certain web pages

Safari Reader

Safari Reader is a brilliant feature that enables web articles to be displayed without ads or clutter, so you can read away without distractions. Not all web pages support this feature, but those that do are instantly apparent because a small 'Reader' icon will be displayed in the address bar at the top of the window.

When you see the Reader icon, tap on it to activate the Safari Reader feature and a new window will be opened that strips away all of the ads, links and unnecessary clutter to leave pure, simple text

Sharing options
Tapping this icon will allow you to add bookmarks, add to Reading List, add to Home Screen, email links, Tweet and Print

Address bar
If you know a website address then type it directly in here. If the page is available for Safari Reader, then the Reader icon will appear in the bar

Tabbed pages
Tap the '+' icon to keep your current page as a tab and open a new tab. You can keep up to nine pages tabbed

Search engine
By default, the Google search engine is built into Safari and used by it, but you can change this in the Settings app

To delete pages from your Reading List, swipe left on the list and tap on the Delete button

that can be read and digested easily (Fig 3). You can also change the font through Safari Reader to make it even bigger and easier to read. To do this, tap the font icon in the top-left corner of the Safari Reader page and choose between the default or enhanced font. When you have finished reading an article through Safari Reader, simply tap on the Reader icon again to return to the original page and continue your browsing as normal.

Offline Reading List

Reading List was first introduced with the release of iOS 5 and it allowed you to save links to web pages for you to read later. However, this was essentially just a glorified bookmark system and it was only with the release of iOS 6 that this feature became truly useful. When you add pages to your Reading List now, Safari will save the entire web page, not just the link, so you can catch up on your reading even when you can't connect to the internet.

To save an article to your Reading List, tap the sharing icon to the left of the address bar in the main Safari window while the page you wish to save is displayed in the main window and then select the Add to Reading List option. To then access the pages saved to

Add a page to your Reading list

1 Tap sharing icon
While on a page, tap the sharing icon and choose 'Add to Reading List'.

2 Access your list
Tap on the bookmarks icon and choose Reading List.

Add Home screen links

1 Go to the webpage
First, access the page you wish to save in your Safari web browser.

2 Tap options
Next, tap the Share icon situated next to the address bar window.

3 Add to Home Screen
Tap on the Add to Home Screen option and name the bookmark.

4 Access easily
Finish by tapping Add. The site will appear on your Home screen.

Safari

your Reading List, tap the book icon at the top of the window, tap Bookmarks and then you will see the Reading List section at the top of your bookmarks list.

Bookmarks bar

As we have explored, there are numerous ways to save and store your favourite web pages to keep them close at hand – and one of the best ways is to save them to your Bookmarks Bar. This is essentially a spread of bookmarked sites that run across the top of your Safari web browser, underneath the address bar, that you can access far quicker than scrolling through your Bookmarks Menu.

To add a new bookmark to your Bookmarks bar, tap the sharing icon to the left of the Safari address bar and then choose the Add

Sharing icon
Tap the sharing icon to access a wide range of Safari features, including the option to print pages

Add to Reading List
With iOS 6 or better, you can save entire web pages to read offline later when you don't have a connection

Social interaction
If you are logged into Twitter and Facebook accounts you can post links to pages in-app

Add to Home Screen
By selecting this option you can turn web pages into app icons on your Home screen for quick access

To share a page via Twitter or Facebook, sign into your account(s) in the Settings app

Bookmark option. You can then rename it and then choose a destination to save it to (Fig 4). Tap the Bookmarks section and then select Bookmarks Bar and when you are happy to add the site, tap Save and the name of the site will appear at the top of your Safari window for easy access.

Share a website

Sometimes you may see something on the web that amazes or outrages you to the extent that you simply have to share it with others. Thankfully, Safari provides a few options to quickly share your online discoveries with others. These options are all accessible through the sharing icon, situated to the left of the address bar which, as we have already discovered, is your gateway to a host of Safari features. From this menu you can select the Mail Link to this Page option, Tweet or Print. The first option enables you to send an email of the page link directly out from Safari without having to copy and paste anything into the Mail app. The title of the link forms the subject of the email and you will be able to add your own message in the main email window, which also contains a link to the site that the recipients can click or tap on.

Sharing a web page

1 Tap share
Tap the sharing icon and then choose a method of sharing.

2 Pass it on
You will be able to share the page without leaving the Safari app.

Enable private browsing

1 Go to Settings
Quit Safari and, from your Home screen, launch your Settings app.

2 Tap Safari
Go to the Safari section from the list on the left of the screen.

3 Go private
Under Privacy, turn on the Private Browsing option.

4 Private browsing
In Private Browsing mode, the interface of Safari will be black.

Mail

With Apple's versatile Mail app you can send emails and receive every message from every account into one handy inbox

You'll use it to…

Link accounts
You can activate the Mail app with any valid email address and password

Send and receive
Keep up to date with email arrivals and quickly send out new messages

Manage accounts
Add as many accounts as you like

Organise your messages
Store and save messages safely away

Find emails easily
Mark certain people as VIPs to access their emails from a special mailbox

Get emails quick
No need to press anything, just get your emails downloaded automatically

Manage your email

Your iPad's built-in Mail app is brilliant for sending and receiving emails, so you don't have to carry a laptop everywhere with you to keep in touch! You can also get all of your different email accounts linked to the app so every email from every account is streamed into one handy inbox, so you'll never have to worry about missing an important one again (Fig 1).

Link an account

If you are using the Mail app for the first time then you will need to set up and tether an account to the app. This is a quick and easy process that requires no more than a valid and active email address and an account password (Fig 2). Once set up, select your account in the 'Inboxes' section of the Mailbox column and then all new messages will instantly be downloaded for that account. You can

Fig 1 Every one of your email accounts, together at last

Fig 2 Once you have set up an account, go to the Settings app to link more accounts to your Mail app

determine when all new emails are pushed from the servers to your mailbox by launching your Settings app, tapping on the Mail, Contacts, Calendars section and then selecting the Fetch New Data option. Activate the Push function and then determine exactly when the messages will be received. To ensure that you get all new mail as soon as possible, tick the 'Manually' option to get all new mail pushed straight to your device as and when. Your device will also now automatically scan for new mail when you launch the app.

Mail and Notifications

One of the many good things about the Mail app is that you don't have to manually press a button to download new messages from the server, it just happens automatically whenever you open the app. What's more, if you have the Mail app listed in your Notification Center then you will get alerts on your screen whenever a new email is received. You should also ensure that Mail is activated in iCloud Settings so that all of your messages – received and read – are synced to all of your devices.

Write and send an email

Writing and sending emails is easy through the intuitive Mail app interface. To compose and send an email, simply tap on the pen and paper icon in the top-right corner of the Mail interface and a blank email will appear. Fill in the recipient's email address, enter a subject and some body text and then hit the 'Send' button. You can also mail out attachments, such as photos and documents from within the other respective apps by tapping on the sharing icon (which is represented by a small rectangle icon with an arrow in it).

You can move emails to different mailboxes by tapping the file icon at the top of the interface

Search for an email

1 Tap Search
While in Mail, tap on the search field at the top-left of the inbox.

2 Enter text
Use the keyboard to type in some keywords to search for.

3 Set criteria
Use the 'From', 'To', 'Subject' or 'All' tabs to focus your search.

4 Results
Emails containing matches will be listed. Check to find the right one.

Mail

Fig 3 Go to Mail, Contacts, Calendars in Settings and then tap 'Add Account…' to include a new mailbox

Manage multiple accounts

It's very rare these days that folk just have one email address. At the very least, most would have a work and a personal account. The Mail app is versatile enough to incorporate virtually any type of email account within a few easy steps and, handily, you can stream all of your mail from all of your accounts into onto main inbox, making it easy to track all aspects of your life simultaneously. To add a new account, launch your Settings app and then go to the Mail, Contacts, Calendars section.

Under the Accounts section at the top of the page you'll see the option to 'Add Account…' (Fig 3). Tap this and then choose the type of account you will be adding – these include Gmail, Yahoo!, AOL, Hotmail and more. Once you have selected the account, enter a name, email address and password for that account and, after a few seconds of verification, the account will be added to your active

VIP
A more recent addition to iPad, iOS 6 users can add certain senders to a VIP mailbox, to keep high-importance emails separate

Inbox
Tap here to see all your received emails. If you have multiple accounts then this option will say 'All Mailboxes' instead

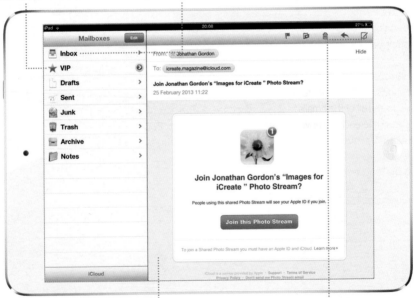

Your emails
When you tap on an email it will be displayed in the main window, whereby you can archive, delete or reply to it

Composing emails
Tap on this icon to start composing a new email. Your address will show up in accordance with the account you are using

To remove people from your VIP list, tap on the sender and then choose 'Remove from VIP'

Mark or flag messages

1 Go to inbox
While in a mailbox, highlight a message in the list to the left.

inboxes within the Mail app. Within the Mail app, you can tap on an individual mailbox to view only the emails relevant to that account, or you can tap on All Inboxes to view all of your received emails in one handy stream.

VIP Mailboxes

With the launch of iOS 6, Apple redesigned Mail with a more streamlined interface for easier reading and writing. One of the new features is VIP Mailboxes. You can now set up a VIP list so that you'll never miss an important email – whether it's from your boss, your best friend or your accountant. To mark a person as a VIP, all you have to do it tap on their email address in a received message and then, on the Sender screen, select the 'Add to VIP' option. A star will then appear next to that person's email address to confirm that they have been marked as a VIP. This star will also be present next to all emails received from that person in your inbox. You can also find VIP emails quickly thanks to your new VIP inbox – just tap on this mailbox and all of the emails from all of your VIPs will be stored there for easy reference. So now you don't have to search your entire inbox for an important message, just go to your VIP mailbox.

2 Tap Edit
Tap the Edit button in the top-left corner of the column.

3 Tap to tick
Place a tick next to the message and then tap Mark.

Mark a person as a VIP

1 Highlight sender
From your inbox, open an email and then tap on the sender.

2 Place a star
Tap 'Add to VIP' and all emails from that person will go to your VIP inbox.

4 Choose option
You can now choose to Flag or Mark as Read.

Calendar

You'll never miss an important event again with the iPad's built-in date-keeper

You'll use it to...

Schedule events
Create new events for yourself and others

Plan ahead
View calendars by day, week, month or year

Sync with other devices
Get key dates from your other desktop calendars imported

Manage calendars
Activate or disable individual calendars

Get alerts
Set reminders for key events

Add birthdays
Import birthdays and anniversaries from your Contacts app

Keep up to date in Calendar

Your iPad's Calendar app is an intuitive way to keep up to date with events for the day, week, month or indeed the next 50+ years, and scheduling event dates into the app is as easy as selecting a calendar view and tapping on a time segment (Fig 1).

Schedule appointments

Making appointments is a quick and easy process in the Calendar app. Use the tabs at the top of the interface to select the 'Day' view and you will see the current day broken down into hourly time segments. To choose a future day, tap on the day in the monthly calendar to the left and a breakdown of the day will be presented on the right-hand side of the interface. You can swipe up or down to scroll through the selected day and then to start scheduling an appointment by pressing and holding on the desired time segment. A New Event banner will then appear on the time segment, quickly

Fig 1 With the Calendar app you can schedule events and appointments far into the future

Fig 2 Press and hold on a time segment to bring up a box that lets you add numerous details to your event

followed by an Add Event box (Fig 2). Here you can enter a title and location for your appointment or event and then factor in the start and end times. Using the other options in this box, you can then choose to repeat the event, invite people from your contacts, trigger alert reminders, add it to a particular calendar and add notes. Tap the Done button when all of the information has been added.

Changeable views

When you launch the app you will see a variety of different views, accessible by tabs at the top of the interface. By default the view is set to Day, with the current day broken down into one-hour segments, but you can easily tap on a different tab to view the calendar by Week, Month, Year or List. In Month view you don't see the timing of each scheduled event, but you can easily spot your busiest days. The List view displays your daily calendar with a list of all commitments for the month to the left of it.

Multiple calendars

One of the best things about the Calendar app is its versatility in allowing you to create different calendars for different areas of your life – such as personal and work – which you can then merge into one main calendar or deactivate them at will via the Calendars menu. You can create new calendars in the desktop Calendar app on your Mac (by clicking the File menu and choosing New Calendar). Any new calendars that you create can then be synced to your iPad Calendar app via iCloud. This should happen automatically but you can speed up the process by tapping the sync button at the top of the Calendars menu.

You can also start scheduling new events by tapping the '+' button in the bottom corner

Create an event

1 Find the date
Use the view tabs to find the date you wish to schedule on.

2 Scroll to time
Swipe up or down through the Day view to find the start time.

3 Press and hold
Add details into the Add Event box that appears.

4 Enter details
Enter locations and start and end times and then hit 'Done'.

Calendar

Fig 3 Tap on the Calendars button and ensure that the Birthdays calendar is activated in the list

Sync birthdays and anniversaries

As you would expect from a built-in iOS app, Calendars works in perfect unison with other apps to make your life easier. In this instance, Calendar works with your Contacts app to display birthdays and anniversary dates that you have assigned to specific people within your Contacts database.

Ensure that you have birthdays assigned to people in your Contacts database and then, in your Calendar app, tap on the Calendars button in the top-left corner of the interface. Scroll down to the 'Other' section, where you will see Birthdays and then ensure that this option is selected (Fig 3). All birthdays and anniversaries assigned in your Contacts app will now be displayed as all-day events on the corresponding day in your calendar. To assign birthdays and anniversaries to specific people on Contacts, tap on a

Your calendars
Tap on the Calendars button to view all of your active calendars and those that you subscribe to. You can manage your calendars from here

Invitations
If you have been invited to a special event from someone else's calendar, then the details will be accessible from here

Calendar views
The row of tabs at the top of the interface will allow you to view calendars by Day, Week, Month, Year and List. Tap on a tab to change the view

Events
A breakdown of the day shows all scheduled events. Tap on an event to view or edit the details

You can also add events to a calendar by importing a calendar (.ics) file from an email

contact and then choose Edit. Scroll down to 'Add Field' and tap '+', then scroll down and choose to add either a Birthday or Date before factoring in the dates concerned.

Manage multiple calendars

Through the Calendar app you can subscribe to any calendar that uses the iCalendar (.ics) format. Many calendar-based services support calendar subscriptions, including iCloud, Yahoo! and Google, it's just a case of hunting around for the right ones.

To subscribe to a calendar, go to your Settings app and then choose the Mail, Contacts, Calendars option. Under Accounts, tap 'Add Account...' and then choose 'Other'. From here you can select the 'Add Subscribed Calendar' option.

You can also subscribe to iCal (or other .ics) calendars published on the web by tapping on a link to the calendar. As we have mentioned, you can also create new calendars in your Mac desktop calendar app and then sync them to your iPad via iCloud. To manage your calendars, tap the Calendars button in the top-left corner of the interface and a list will display all available calendars that you can then enable or disable at will.

Subscribe to new calendars online

1 Find calendar
Search for iCal calendars online and then hit the Subscribe button.

2 Activate new calendar
The calendar will be added and can then be activated from the list.

Set event alerts

1 Tap on event
Tap on an existing event or create a new one by pressing '+'.

2 Tap on Alert
Scroll down the event box and then tap on the Alert option.

3 Select a time
From the list, select an option for when you want to be alerted.

4 Tap Done
Now tap on 'Done' and then your iPad will automatically alert you.

You'll use it to…

Access Contacts
Maintain personal and business details

Edit Contacts
Add and delete details

Search Contacts
Access your contacts quickly

Address emails quickly
Open an email from the Contacts section

Sync contacts
Transfer Contacts to multiple devices

Assign photos
Attach a photo to a contact for visual recognition of a person

Contacts

With the Contacts app, you can access and edit your contact lists from personal, business and organisational accounts

Manage your contacts

Contacts allow you to not only access your friends and associates but you can edit them from a selection of personal and business accounts. You can also search for details within thanks to a easy search field and send emails by clicking on an address (Fig 1).

Add, edit and delete Contacts

To add a contact on the iPad you need to tap the Contacts app, which will open the Contacts window. This displays a list of contacts, in alphabetical order, on the left hand side of the screen with the intimate details of each contact displayed on the right hand side of the screen.

To Edit your contact database and add a new contact, tap the '+' button situated in the centre at the bottom of the screen. A new screen will open up displaying an empty template which you can

Fig 1 (above) You can use the Contacts information within other apps, adding efficiency and convenience

Fig 2 (right) To enter data on each template line, touch the line and enter data via the iPad's floating keyboard

fill in via the pop-up keyboard present at the base of the screen (Fig 2). When you have completed the page, press Done to close the record and return to the index. To edit an existing record, press the Edit button situated in the centre at the bottom of the screen. This time, the completed template will be present with options to either change the text or delete entire lines of information using the swivelling red buttons that turn into delete buttons when touched.

Add extra information to your contacts

When you access the edit screen for a contact, you are presented with a standard template array that asks you basic information. You can, however, add further information if you wish which is not readily observable from the basic edit page. To see it, you have to press the '+' key, which will bring a pop-up box displaying a wide choice of extra fields, including Twitter information, nickname, Instant Message information, birthday and related people.

Contacts & iCloud

Keep your contact details, including your mail contacts, up-to-date across all your devices (including a MacBook or other laptop, iMac or PC or iPhone) with the iCloud storage facility.

Contacts are stored in your iCloud account and pushed wirelessly to your other iOS devices and computers that are set up with the same iCloud account. To make sure that the iCloud and Contacts are working together, go to Settings app on your iPad and tap the iCloud section on the left hand side of the screen. On the right hand side of the screen, swipe the button next to the Contacts header to On.

If your iCloud storage is insufficient to store your Contact information, you can purchase more

Assign a photo to a particular contact

1 Edit mode
Enter the Contacts app and tap on a new or current contact.

2 Add a photo
If it is not visible, scroll to the Add Photo box and tap on it.

3 Take or choose
Via the menu, choose to either Take Photo or Choose Photo.

4 Insert photo
Use the iPad to take a photo or import from your photo archive.

Contacts

Integrate with other apps

It is possible to integrate the Contacts apps with other apps to form a seamless connection and also to allow you to perform tasks without having to pause to copy and paste from one app to another, or pause while one program is stopped and another opened. A good example is the Maps app.

If you open a current contact which features a full address, just tap on the address and this action will automatically open the Maps app (Fig 3). The Maps screen will then be displayed and that app will attempt to provide a visual indication of the address itself, giving you information on the location but also providing you with the opportunity to set up directions from your current location to that address. Similarly, if you list a website within the Contacts app,

Fig 3 Tapping on a contact's address will open the Maps app and take you to that particular location

Extra fields
This field enables you to type whatever extra information you need, like Twitter names and job titles

Template
Type new information or edit the current information within the boxes. Scroll down to see more options

Delete info
When editing a contact, press on a red circle to reveal the Delete button, then tap it to clear the field

Linking contacts
Press here in order to link and unlink the contacts that you want this information to be associated with

Before you share your contact, make sure all of the info is correct and edit it if you need to

tapping on it will open the Safari browser and the contents of that website will be displayed. You can also tap on an email address within your contact list to open the Mail app and create a new email to send to that person.

Share a contact

Within each completed Contact page, you have the ability to share the contact. This provides a quick and simple way of sharing details, which is ideal if a contact is packed with information that would take too long to copy or rewrite.

To share your contact, open your desired Contact page and scroll to the base of the page. On the right hand side of the sheet, tap on the Share Contact button. Two options then appear denoting how you can share that contact information. In this case, Email and Message. Tap on the Email option, for example, and a new email page will appear. Notice that a file icon also exists. This .vcf file contains all of the required information. When you email this file, your recipient can then load it into their Contacts app. All of the information will then be made available to the recipient too, so your Contacts app is a great way of networking.

Share via Message

1 Open Contact
Open a contact and scroll to the bottom until you see 'Share Contact'.

2 Share contact
Tap on Share Contact, select Message, enter the text and then send.

Email a contact card

1 Open Contacts
Open the Contacts app and select the contact of choice.

2 Scroll to Contacts
Scroll down until you reach the Share Contact option. Tap on it.

3 New email page
Tap on the Email option and a new email page will appear.

4 Complete email
Complete the email and send to pass on the .vcf file.

Messages

Use the Messaging app and keep in contact with your friends and family

You'll use it to…

Send text messages
Send unlimited text messages to other OS X and iOS devices over Wi-Fi or 3G

Share photos
You can send photos via a text message

Share videos
Pass your videos on to others

Add attachments
Any attached data can be texted

Have conversations
Your texts can be grouped into a conversation template

Chat with groups
You can send one message to a group of people

Keep in touch using texts

Messaging is one of the most popular activities within the mobile sphere. Using your iPad's Messages app, you can send text to one or more people, often simultaneously along with a variety of data attachments, in a similar way to email (Fig 1).

Text using iMessage

The concept of messaging between mobile phones is not unusual but Apple has moved the technology on a step by introducing the iMessage. The difference between the basic text message and the iMessage is that you can begin a conversation on one device and then continue it on another device (Fig 2). For example, you can start an iMessage conversation on your iPhone while travelling on a bus, but then when you get home and you have entered your home office to check a document on your iPad, you can continue the conversation on that device without losing the flow.

Fig 1 (above) Messages are grouped into conversations to enable you to retain the structure and flow of the chats

Fig 2 (right) Thanks to iCloud you can begin a conversation on one device and then continue ti on another

78

As long as the devices are both logged into the same iCloud account, the conversation will, in fact, be available on all of the iOS devices that you currently own, giving you a high degree of flexibility. If you are concerned about security, be assured that all iMessages are encrypted.

Share photos

One of the highlights of the messaging system, on the iPad, is the ability to transfer data along with your text. One of the data types that you can send is the photo. To do that you need to choose your required contact and write a covering note. To choose an image, tap on the camera icon to the left of the message input window and then you can either take a new photo from within the Messages app by selecting the Take Photo or Video option (after which your iPad's Camera app will launch), or import one from your Photos app by selecting the Choose Existing option. If you go for the latter option, scroll through your various photo albums to find the images you wish to attach.

Send locations

One of the unique aspects of messaging is not only having the ability to send an object in the form of data but being able to send links to other data too. Hence, you can send a link to the location of a map, for example.

To do that, click on Maps and find the location you wish to share. Press on the location to trigger the banner heading, press 'i' for more information, scroll down the pop-up window and select Share Location, then, from the sharing menu, choose Message.

Sharing your location also reveals a useful distance-from-your-current-location figure

Delete messages

1 Select contact
Find the contact or conversation you want to edit.

2 Edit conversation
Select the Edit icon, to the right of the contact name.

3 Select message
Choose a message by pressing the empty circle next to it.

4 Delete message
Press the Delete button, at the base of the screen.

Messages

Group messaging

There is an alternative messaging method which can often save time and effort. Your iPad provides the ability to send a single message to a group of people. To begin, load the Message app and open a new message. Complete the message and press the '+' icon next to the 'To' header at the top of the screen (Fig 3). Your Contacts list will then pop on screen.

This list can be scrolled in order for you to find the group of contacts you wish to choose. Select the first person you wish to send your email, which will be inserted as a sender. Tap the '+' icon again to select another and repeat until your group is complete. If you receive a Message as part of a group chat, the conversation's

Edit button
Tap this button to erase entire conversations. Press the associated red button and tap Delete

New message
Tap the pad and pencil icon to bring up a new message screen, then type your message

Delete text
Tap the arrow icon at the top-right-hand side of the screen to delete individual messages from the app

Contacts
Tap to either send a message, enter a FaceTime conversation or Share a Contact

You can share a contact from the Message app. Click on the 'head' icon, then tap Share Contact

entry in the Messages app will have the group icon (which looks like the silhouette of two people) to the left of it. It's easy to tell which participant sent the message, even in a group chat because the person's name will appear above the message itself when you look at the conversation.

Read/delivery receipts

We are all used to sending text messages to colleagues, friends and family and, when the text leaves our phone, we get on with our lives. There are times, however, when an important message is sent and you want to be sure that the other person knows you have read it. This may be because of a business decision or maybe you just want to make sure that the recipient is aware that a message has been read.

On the iPad, you can turn on the Send Read Receipts option which will provide the sender with an indication that you have received and have read the message. To do this, tap on the Settings app and then scroll the left window until you reach the Messages section. Tap Messages and, on the right, a new window will appear. Now look for the Send Read Receipts option and turn it on.

Enable read receipts

1 Settings
Go to the Settings>Messages and then turn 'Send Read Receipts' to on.

2 Get the confirmation
As soon as your message is read, you'll see confirmation under the message.

Add more addresses

1 Launch Settings
Launch the Settings app from the Home screen of your iPad.

2 Send & Receive
Go to the Messages section and tap on Send & Receive.

3 Another Email
Choose the option labelled Add Another E-mail.

4 Type address
Type in the secondary email address you'd like to use.

Reminders

You need never forget to do something ever again with your iPad's built-in memory bank

You'll use it to…

Make lists
Compose lists of tasks to complete

Set reminders
Get alerted when you need to complete particular tasks

Sync to iCloud
Get reminders pushed to other devices

Tick off tasks
A handy check-box lets you tick off items as you complete them

Check your calendar
Reminders syncs with the Calendar app to track your key dates

Remember everything
An intuitive interface means reminding yourself is easy

Set and schedule tasks

Reminders lets you organise your life, setting yourself tasks complete with due dates and lists (Fig 1). The app works with iCloud and your calendar accounts, so any changes that you make will update automatically on all of your iOS devices and computers. It's the simple way to never forget anything ever again!

Set a reminder

Setting yourself a new reminder is a quick and easy process and you can tap the '+' button to get started. You will now be prompted to enter a description of your task, so use the pop-up keyboard to summarise your task and then press the down arrow to make the keyboard disappear. You can then fine-tune the settings for the task by tapping on it in the list (Fig 2).

When the Details box appears, tap on the Remind Me button and then move the 'On a Day' slider to the On position. Now tap

Fig 1 (above) With Reminders you can organise your life into simple 'to-do' lists

Fig 2 (right) Create a task and tap on it to bring up the Details box

on the date and you will be able set it to any date and time you want. Once you have set the remind date, tap Done to return to the Details box and then select the Show More option. Here you can select a list for your reminder to appear on and add any additional notes that you want.

Create lists

Organising reminders into lists makes it easy to keep your work, personal and other to-dos separate from each other. The app comes with one list for active reminders, plus a built-in list of completed items – and you can also add other lists of your own. To create a list, tap on the 'List' tab at the top of the interface and then tap Edit. The option to Create New List will then appear under your various accounts, so tap on one and then type in the name of the list.

Reminders and iCloud

Reminders is just one of many apps that utilises Apple's iCloud service, which means that any lists and tasks that you create in the iCloud section will be synced and pushed to all of your other iOS devices and computers wirelessly.

Obviously it might not be possible to carry your iPad around with you everywhere, so to get reminders created on iPad pushed to your iPhone would be useful. Go to Settings and ensure that the Reminders slider is turned on in the iCloud Settings to use this feature. With iOS 6, the ability to set location based reminders was also added so that your device will chime in when you either leave or arrive at a certain address.

To delete lists, in List view, tap Edit and then hit the red '-' icon for each list you want to delete

Repeat reminders

1 Open the app
Open your Reminders app, and press the plus in the top-right.

2 Write reminder
You can now write your reminder and it will appear in your list.

3 Details
Once finished, tap the reminder and it'll bring up the details.

4 Repeat
Turn on Remind Me On a Day to set the reminder to repeat.

Notes

Use Notes to jot down your thoughts, new ideas or to act as a reminder for useful information

You'll use it to…

Write down ideas
Jot ideas while you're on the move

Organise automatically
Notes are listed by time and date created

Take advantage of iCloud
Share your notes and information

Keep note accounts
Create a note-specific account

Search your notes
Search the app for a specific note

Print and email
You can print your notes via AirPlay

Take notes with ease

The Notes app is the perfect way to quickly write down those ideas, lists and anything else that pops into your head that you may need to remember later on (Fig 1). The Notes app also gives you all sorts of options for moving your notes to different locations and platforms, so you'll never forget anything ever again.

Write and share notes

You can create a new note by tapping the + icon in the top-right corner of the screen and all of your notes are automatically stored. Every note you create will be presented in an easily accessible list and anything you write down in the Notes app is simple to share with others from within the app itself.

To start sharing your notes, tap the Sharing icon that's located at the bottom of the screen (indicated by an arrow in a box) and you will then be presented with options to Email, Message, Copy or Print

Fig 1 (above) Notes provides plenty of screen space for you to write down and store a whole range of information

Fig 2 (right) You can easily share your Notes in a variety of different ways

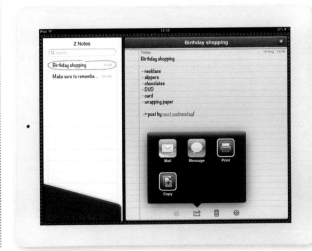

(Fig 2). If you opt to email your note, the contents of the current note will be copied and pasted into an email. All you have to do then is add the recipient's address in the correct field and you can mail it straight out from within the Notes app. There's no need to cut, paste and switch between the apps yourself. You can print your notes wirelessly, and Notes is also iCloud compatible. Any notes you create can be accessed on all iOS devices.

Keyboard tricks

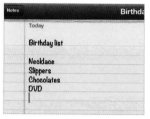

There are plenty of tricks and shortcuts that you can also use to your advantage. Pressing the space bar twice in quick succession will place a full stop and a space at the end of your sentence. Also, press and hold on the numbers key and quickly slide your finger to the number or symbol you wish to place before taking your finger off – it will switch back to the letters keyboard, allowing you to continue typing. To get a quick apostrophe, tap and hold the '!' button and slide your finger upwards.

Notes and iCloud

Notes can be linked to the iCloud. This gives you the ability to access your notes via different platforms such as a MacBook, iPhone and iMac as well as your iPad. If you use a **me.com** or **mac.com** email address for iCloud, go to the Settings and tap on iCloud and turn on Notes. If you use a Gmail or other web email account for iCloud, go to the Settings app and tap on the Mail option then tap Contacts and Calendars. Then turn on Notes for the account. All of these features enhance your Notes experience and make note-taking as simple as possible.

Enable Caps Lock in the Settings app and then activate it by double-tapping the Shift key

Change the Notes font

1 Settings Tap Settings on the main screen, then scroll down to the Notes section.

2 General Tap the Notes button and a new window will appear on the right of the screen.

3 Font Note the three fonts listed at the top of the screen. Tap on the font you wish to use.

4 Return Go back to the Notes screen and notice that the new font has changed.

Maps

Use the Maps app to search for and find directions to a location in both graphical or textual form

You'll use it to…

Enter a search
Search for and find your chosen location

Driving
Get a great series of driving directions

Flyover
Obtain a 3D, aerial flyover view

Zoom in
Double-tap on a map to zoom in

More info
Press on a label to find out more info

Print
Print out a useful set of directions straight from the iPad

Find your way around the world

Maps on your iPad provides you with a real-time map that can offer turn-by-turn directions that are spoken by the iPad. Alongside this there are interactive 3D views plus an amazing Flyover feature. The entire world is open for examination and you can use the spread gesture to zoom in too, for even more detail (Fig 1).

Navigating Maps

To navigate around the Maps app, all you have to do is tap the search field and then type an address to go to your desired location.

You can also go to a location at the same time as inserting other information, such as an intersection in the USA (8th and Market) or an area in London (Westminster) or a landmark in Australia (Sydney Opera House) (Fig 2). You can even enter a postcode and business type that is close to your current location such as 'movies' or 'restaurants near me'.

Fig 1 (above) If you want to jump between global points, it's easy to rotate the Earth over multiple axes

Fig 2 (right) The items located in your search are highlighted by red pins

You will also notice that, as you enter the search field, a long list of other suggestions will appear in a drop-down box, connected with your search text. You can tap on those too.

To navigate the actual maps, you can move up or down, left or right, drag the screen or rotate the map using two fingers on the screen. You will find a compass appearing in the upper-right corner to show the map's orientation. You can then return to the north-facing orientation by tapping on the compass icon again.

Get directions

Once you have found your required location, press on the pin to reveal the banner. Then press the Directions button on the top left-hand corner of the screen. A drop-down window will reveal your chosen location and three modes of transport: walking, car and bus.

Once you have selected how you want to travel, press the Route button on the top right-hand side of the window and a visual route will appear on the map.

Turn-by-turn navigation

You need cellular data to make the most of this feature. Tap the Directions button on the top-left of the screen and then tap the mode of transport that you wish to use. Enter the start and end locations, then tap Route or choose a location or a route from the list. Maps follows your progress as you go and speaks turn-by-turn directions to guide you towards your destination. To show or hide the controls, tap the screen. You can view the turn-by-turn directions by tapping Start, then swiping on the instruction left to see the next instruction.

Press the Overview button on the top right-hand corner to get a view of the whole route

Bookmark a place

1 Route Select your start and end point and then tap on Route to see a visual representation.

2 End point Press on your final location to reveal a banner. This will feature the name.

3 Information Press the banner to see further information about the location. A window appears.

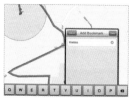

4 Bookmark At the base is the Add To Bookmarks button. Press here to save.

Maps

Flyover

With the new Flyover feature in Maps, you can see a selection of major metro areas from the air with photorealistic, interactive 3D views (Fig 3). The feature is not available for the entire planetary surface, but more cities are constantly being added and updated.

   The feature enables you to explore cities in high resolution via zoom, pan, tilt and rotate gestures. To use the Flyover you should zoom into your desired location until the Flyover mode becomes active. You can tell if Flyover mode is available because you will be able to tap the building button on the bottom-left of the screen.

   Alternatively, you can drag two fingers up the screen to tilt the 3D building effect. This gesture command adjusts the camera angle. Use other gesture commands to navigate around the map.

Fig 3 The Flyover feature can produce some highly complex 3D objects

Directions
Placed on the top left-hand corner, tap here to generate locations to and from a place

Search bar
On the top right-hand side is the search bar to search for any location in the world

Location
The location is signified by the red pin which, when tapped, triggers a bar than can provide further information

Page corner
Under the bottom right-hand page corner lie the map type, print and Show Traffic options

After selecting your style, you can return to the map page by pressing on the screen

As you move around the map, depending on the complexity of the map surface and the number of buildings present, you may see some slight delays as the 3D objects are built on the grid surface by the iPad. We don't recommend using Flyover on a cellular data connection – it'll be slow to load and will eat into your data plan.

Standard, Hybrid, and Satellite map views
When you are viewing a map location, there are three main ways that this information can be presented to you. If you want to see the most realistic view on the location, then you should select the Satellite view. This produces a bird's-eye view point on the ground and is the most realistic of the three, showing true-to-life features such as major landmarks and landscapes plus rivers and roads.

On the other end of the scale is the Standard view, which provides you with a similar view as you might see on a paper map. This includes road names plus the names of areas and indications of landmarks such as parks, schools, shopping centres and much more. The Hybrid view utilises the satellite landscape but inserts the standard-view labelling to give you a blend that mixes the realistic with the informative that might be better suited to some.

Access the different map views

1 The corner Press the bottom-right-hand corner of the map to expose the map styles menu.

2 Change the style There are three map styles revealed under the map page. Choose one to use.

Overlay traffic data

1 Drop a pin Tap the 'Directions' tab and then drop a pin at a location to get the route.

2 Go to options Tap on the curled page corner at the bottom-right of the screen.

3 Turn on the traffic Move the 'Traffic' overlay slider to the 'On' position and return to the map.

4 See congestion Areas of traffic congestion will be marked in traffic light colours on the roads.

Siri

Siri is a voice-command interface system, an intelligent personal assistant for new iPads

You'll use it to…

Go hands free
Give voice commands to your iPad

Speak naturally
Siri understands natural speech

Set functions
Set an alarm or similar utility by voice

Open apps
Ask Siri to open any app for you

Get directions
Find directions via the Maps app

Communicate socially
Post messages to Twitter and Facebook

Your personal assistant

With Siri, a voice-controlled interface that uses natural speech to initiate commands, you can write and send a message, schedule a meeting or place a FaceTime call. But that's not all, you can also get directions, set a reminder and search the web. It's not available for the original iPad or iPad 2.

Search the web with Siri

To start Siri, enter the Settings section and tap on General. Then tap on Siri to enter the Siri-specific settings. Swipe the switch to the On position. Siri is now enabled (Fig 1).

To activate the Siri interface, press the Home button until Siri appears on the screen. You'll hear two beeps and see the "What can I help you with?" text appear on the screen. Give the Siri interface your web search command using speech (Fig 2). The microphone icon will light up. Talking with Siri can be continued by

Fig 1 (above) You can enable the Siri interface by entering the Settings section

Fig 2 (right) Requesting a web page automatically loads the browser software and loads your requested page

tapping on the microphone icon. The interface then waits for you to stop speaking. If you have completed your command, tap the microphone icon to end. This action is recommended when there is background noise to contend with, and It can also speed up your conversation with Siri.

After you have stopped talking, the Siri interface displays what it has heard and it will then respond to your query. You will be taken to your browser where your requested web page will load with your search results.

Send an email with Siri

1 Start Siri Press the Home key for a few seconds to open up the Siri interface.

Get directions with Siri

Before you can get directions from Siri, you need to tap Settings and scroll down to the Privacy section. Tap Privacy to open the window on the right. The Location Services should be On. Look down to the Siri switch and turn that to the On position. Press the Home button until Siri appears, then give your direction instructions. The interface will then open the Maps app and provide you with a full set of visual and aural directions.

Create family links

You can teach Siri about yourself by constantly using it. Siri learns and expands its database on you to make its operation easier and more efficient. Siri also obtains its information from your personal info card (My Info) in the Contacts app. If you tap Settings>General>Siri>My Info then tap your name, Siri can learn from your family links, so put those relationships on your info card. If you tell Siri to text your sister, Siri asks you who your sister is and then adds that relationship to your personal info card.

2 Send email If you ask Siri to Send Email, it will respond with a recipient request.

3 Email content Tell Siri who you want to send it to and state its contents.

Ask Siri a trivia question and it should have an answer for you, or know somewhere that does

4 Send Tell Siri to send the email message to your contact. Siri will respond once completed.

Fig 3 Siri pulls movie ratings from Rotten Tomatoes when you ask it for reviews

Extra features

With the release of iOS 6, Apple enabled users in the UK to have the same level of functionality as those in the US, namely the ability to search for businesses, restaurants, movies and more in the local area.

By asking Siri what's nearby, such as requesting the closest coffee shops, you will be given a list of establishments and the distances to them. Selecting one of these will bring up more details, including contact numbers and the exact address.

Siri can also provide ratings for movies and show you the listings of what's on at nearby cinemas. The former is especially useful, enabling you to find out what's worth seeing at the moment before

FaceTime
Siri can't make calls yet but it can FaceTime you with whoever you want to talk to

Set reminders
You can set reminders on the fly for a specific date and time by talking to Siri

Send a message
You can dictate a message to Siri and it will then send it to your chosen recipient

Directions
Using Maps, Siri can give you directions between any two locations

Ask Siri what football is on tonight and it will duly oblige by providing you with the fixture list

you check the times. Select the film you want to see and Siri will show you where you can see it.

Also, with regards to sports, Siri will now show you the fixture list for your chosen sport. For example, you can ask for the Premier League listings on the weekend and Siri will show you the teams that are playing and when.

Social networking

Siri now has the ability to post to social networks, so you don't have to open up the individual apps for them. For example, just by saying "send a tweet", Siri will bring up the new post box for Twitter, and you can then tell it what to post from your account. The same can be done for Facebook by telling Siri to post to Facebook instead.

Of course, before you do this you'll need to sign in to your appropriate social networks. To do this, first you'll need to get the relevant app, and then you just go to Settings and sign in.

Apple also has some more new features in store for the future that will make Siri even better. This includes Eyes Free, which integrates Siri with voice control systems, such as you might have in your car, so you can activate it without taking your eyes off the road.

Post to social networks

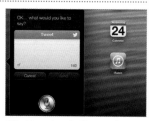

1 Signing in First, you will need to sign in to your social media accounts inside the Settings app.

2 Post to networks Once you've done that, simply tell Siri what you want to post and where.

Find a restaurant

1 Just ask Ask Siri for some restaurants in the area and it'll give you a list.

2 Reservation If Siri can't make a reservation for you, it'll show you how to do it yourself.

3 Information Select one of the restaurants and Siri will show you the contact details.

4 Directions Ask Siri for some directions to the restaurant and it'll show you how to get there.

Clock

Keep track of the time wherever you are in the world and never be late again with the Clock app

You'll use it to…

Browse world times
See the time in cities across the globe

Set an alarm
Have different alarms for numerous tasks

Measure elapsed time
Use the stopwatch and see time go by

Measure time intervals
See the time left between tasks

Catch the latest news
The clock links to Yahoo! in your location

Check the weather
View summaries of local climates

Keep track of time

As well as letting you see the time across the world, the Clock app also allows you to time the interval between events or use a stopwatch (Fig 1). It also operates as a brilliant alarm clock with the possibility of setting multiple alerts.

Set an alarm

When you tap the + icon in the top right-hand corner, you are able to begin setting an alarm (Fig 2). Use the dials to configure the exact time by scrolling up and down using your fingers until you find the right one. You can then decide whether or not you want to repeat the alarm, which you can do on any day of the week, and whether or not you would like to include a snooze function.

It is possible to label that particular alarm with any name you wish. For example, you could decide that you would like to label one 'Waking Up' and another one for a Meeting.

Fig 1 (above) You can add pages and pages of world times – just tap Add

Fig 2 (right) Tap the + icon in order to begin setting up your alarms for various tasks

It is also possible to add a particular sound to your alarm. When you have completed this, the alarm will show on the calendar within the Clock app so that you can see, at a glance, when any of your alarms have been set. It is possible to edit any of these by selecting Edit in the top left-hand corner.

Stopwatch and timers

When you tap on the Stopwatch tab at the bottom of the screen, you are able to begin measuring elapsed time. Likewise, when you

select Timer, you can measure time intervals as well.

With the Stopwatch, you simply tap Start and the time will begin to increase. When you tap Stop, it will cease. The Stopwatch has a great lap timer, too. Tapping Lap when a lap is finished will show the time that the lap took to complete.

On the Timer, simply input the timescale you want using the dials and then tap Start. The countdown begins.

World clocks

As well as being able to see a set of five default time zones of Cupertino, New York, Paris, Beijing and Tokyo, tapping Add lets you find any location around the world and see the exact time at that particular location too.

When you tap the Add button, you will be shown a list of included time zones. You can either scroll through these and find one that you want, or you can decide instead to use the keyboard and input a search term. Tap the result you are looking for and the clock will be added to those that already exist. The time will also be placed on the world map.

You can quickly turn off your alarms by going to Alarm and moving the slider to the Off position

Add music to an alarm

1 Add alarm Tap on the + button to Add Alarm. You will then need to select Sound.

2 Select song Look under the category of Songs; some of your tunes will be listed here.

3 Pick a song Either tap one of these options or, alternatively, select Pick a song.

4 Search for tunes When you have found the one you want to use, tap it to choose it.

FaceTime

FaceTime

FaceTime is ideal for talking to your friends, family or colleagues in real time via video link

You'll use it to…

Make video calls
Talk face to face with friends and family

Talk to other devices
Call from iPad to iPhone or MacBook

Switch cameras
Easily switch from front to rear cameras

Chat for free
FaceTime calls are free of charge

Use FaceTime on TV
Great for making group calls

Add Favourites
Create FaceTime favourites

Chat face-to-face

FaceTime allows you to undertake video calls with another user of a compatible Apple device: iPhone, iPod touch, MacBook and iMac. The app also includes a picture-in-picture facility while you're talking, so you can see how you look to the person on your screen (Fig 1).

Call a contact with FaceTime

To enable you to use FaceTime, you will initially need to set up an Apple ID, if you haven't already obtained one. You'll also need a Wi-Fi connection or cellular 3G link that can connect you to the Internet for the app to work.

When you open FaceTime, you may be prompted to sign in using your Apple ID or to create a new account (Fig 2). Before you can make your FaceTime call, tap the Contacts app and find the details you require. Then choose a name and tap that person's phone number or their email address – either will do to open FaceTime.

Fig 1 You can check your own appearance and control volume during a FaceTime call

Fig 2 Make sure FaceTime is turned on the Settings app first

When making the call, you can move the iPad in either landscape or portrait orientation. It is advisable, however, to lock the rotation before you make your call to avoid disturbing orientation changes during your chat.

If you have recently called a FaceTime contact, you can call them again quickly by visiting the Recents section found within the Phone app. You will see a small video-camera icon placed next to the contact.

Add favourites

Using the FaceTime app is similar, in practice, to using the Phone app. You can make calls, interact with callers, respond to the Recent list of missed calls and so on.

In a similar way, FaceTime will also require, at some point, time-saving additions that will speed up the process. Saving your contacts to a Favourites section, for example, may prove to be useful. To add a favourite, tap + and choose a contact.

Chat on multiple devices

One of the more useful features of the FaceTime app is its ability to be used in between devices. Not just devices of the same type, either. While you can easily utilise FaceTime between iPad and iPad, you can also use it between an iPad and iPhone, iPad and iMac and iPad and MacBook.

There are slight differences in how communication is initiated, however. The requirement of an Apple ID is constant but, in addition, you will need a phone number if you want to call an iPhone. To call an iPad, iPod touch or Mac, you can use an email.

To FaceTime a Favourite from the list, simply tap on the name in the Contacts app

The FaceTime controls

1 Picture in picture Look at the small image of yourself to see what your caller can see.

2 Switch cameras Toggle the camera so that your caller can see what you are seeing.

3 Mute Press the icon at the bottom of the screen. The other person will not hear your words.

4 End call To end the call, press the End button , positioned at the bottom of the screen.

Camera

With the iPad's built-in camera, you have the power to take both photos and video at your fingertips

You'll use it to…

Take photos
Ideal when you're on the move

Record a video
Monitor the video on your screen

Use location services
Tagged images can be used by apps

Take a self-portrait
Take an image of yourself

View images
Examine your photos while on the move

Watch your videos
You can also view your suite of videos

Take photos on the go

If you own an iPad 2 or later, you can take still photos with the built-in camera. You are also able to record videos with the rear-facing camera. The front-facing camera can be used to point at your face for use with FaceTime.

Shoot photos

To take a photo with the iPad you must first open up the Camera app. Then make sure that the Camera/Video switch, situated at the bottom right-hand side of the screen, is set to the Camera mode. To do this, move the switch to the camera icon position.

The next stage is to lift the iPad and aim it at your chosen subject. Make sure that you frame your subject as you want it to appear in the shot, then pause a second (Fig 1). This allows the iPad to focus properly (a rectangle briefly appears where the camera is focusing and setting the exposure).

Fig 1 When taking a photo or recording a video, frame your subject within the screen first

Fig 2 Make sure that the slider is set to the camera icon take a single image

When you photograph people, iPad uses face detection to automatically focus on and balance the exposure across up to ten faces. Tap on the Camera icon that is situated within the screen, half-way up on the right-hand side. When you press, the image will be taken and a shutter sound-effect will be triggered to indicate that an image has been snapped (Fig 2). In addition you'll see an iris animation move across the screen which provides a visual indication that your photograph has been taken.

Take faster and better photographs

Rather than having to press a virtual shutter button every time you want a shot, you can also use the volume buttons when taking photos. It works exactly the same way as the capture icon on the screen, but means you can hold the iPad steady. It is close to the lens, however, so be careful not to place your finger in the wrong position. Also, turn on Grid Lines from the Options to compose your shots correctly.

Share your images

With a little practice, you can take some great images with your iPad. If you want to show these off, you can easily share your stored images with a variety of friends, family and colleagues via email, text message or even a Tweet.

To do this, choose a photo that you wish to send and tap it. A new set of controls will appear. Press the Share icon on the top right-hand corner of the screen. This will reveal a range of icons that will allow you to share your images. Press one of them to activate the app and initiate the share.

Within the share menu, you can also select the Copy icon to copy your image for use elsewhere

Use grid lines

1 Launch the app Launch the Camera app by pressing the Camera icon.

2 Options Press the Options button in the bottom-left to highlight the Grid menu.

3 Swipe When the Grid menu appears, swipe the button to the On position.

4 Arrange image Use the on-screen grid to compose and arrange your image.

Shoot videos

To take a video with your iPad, first open up the Camera app. Then make sure that the Camera/Video switch situated at the bottom right-hand side of the screen is set to the Video mode. When you change the mode from camera to video, the iPad confirms the action by triggering an iris animation which then recedes to reveal a new start icon. Instead of the camera button, this icon is now a simple red dot button.

Lift the iPad and aim it at your chosen subject. Tap on the new red icon that is situated within the screen, half way up on the right-hand side. When you press this button on the iPad, a sound effect will be triggered to indicate the start of the video. When the video is running, a timer will note the passing seconds, at the top right-hand

Fig 3 Record the video and note the passing seconds via the time counter

Slideshow
Press here to initiate the slideshow option of your photo archive, complete with dissolves and music option

Photos
Press this button to return to the Camera Roll section, your photograph storage or archive area

Trash
The Trash Can is present to allow you to quickly dispose of any image or video you no longer want

Bottom strip
The strip at the bottom shows tiny thumbnails of your photos, offering a quick-access facility

In the Edit screen, next to the frame viewer, press the play icon to run the video and view your work

part of the screen (Fig 3). To stop recording your video, press the red button icon again. The saved video will then be placed as a small icon on the bottom left-hand corner. Press this to play back your saved movie sequence.

Edit and trim videos

When you have recorded your videos, you can then edit them by trimming the frames from the beginning and also from the end of a video or from any other video in your Camera Roll album. You can also replace the original video that you have recorded or you can save the newly edited video as a video clip.

To trim your video, play the video to be edited and tap the screen. You'll see a set of controls. At the top of the screen, a frame viewer will appear, exposing all of the individual frames of your video. To trim your video, press and drag one end of the video, then press the yellow Trim button. Once you have done this, a short menu will drop down and ask you if you want to Trim Original or Save A New Clip. If you select the Trim Original option, then the trimmed frames from your sequence will be permanently deleted from the original video.

Save clip

1 Yellow trim To save your video as a new video clip, press the yellow Trim button.

2 Camera Roll Press Save as New Clip. The clip with then be saved in your Camera Roll album.

Find the Camera Roll

1 Access via icon Tap the square icon at the bottom-left to head straight to the Camera Roll.

2 Swipe to view In the Camera app, swipe to the right to see the last photo you took.

3 Lock screen The lock screen's picture icon shows you photos set in Settings>Picture Frame.

4 Access from apps Many apps let you access the Camera Roll to use or manipulate images.

You'll use it to...

View your images
See photographs in stunning clarity

Zoom in on pictures
Use your fingers to get extra detail

See thumbnails
View images at a glance

Share photographs
Send images via social media or mail

Print images
Create a hard copy of any photo

Produce a slideshow
Have images automatically display

Photos

Use this app to keep your precious photos in perfect order and browse them with ease

View your images

Images that you take via screenshots, from the web or using the built-in camera automatically appear within the Photos app. These are then available to you within one handy place, allowing you to scroll through them and see thumbnails for easy access (Fig 1).

The Camera Roll

When you take a photograph using your iPad's camera, it will appear in your Camera Roll, a section in the Photos app on the iPad. It is also possible to see the Camera Roll by opening the Camera app and tapping the icon in the bottom left-hand corner.

If you want to view an image in your Camera Roll, you can do this one of two ways: either go direct to Photos by tapping on the app on the home screen or view your shots via the Camera app. Then tap on one of the images to instantly bring it up on the entire screen and flick left and right to go through them (Fig 2).

Fig 1 (above) All of your images are displayed as thumbnails so you can jump to any photo quickly and easily

Fig 2 (right) You can make photographs appear in the full iPad screen by tapping a thumbnail in the Camera Roll

When viewing a photo or video in the Camera Roll album, you can also tap the screen to bring up some controls. This will allow you to edit, share or even delete an image. You can also go back to your Camera Roll to view the thumbnails again for quick selection.

AirPlay

You can view photographs from the iPad on an Apple TV, a low-priced set-top box for your television. This is done via AirPlay which is built in to your iOS device. Both your iOS and Apple TV devices need to be on the same Wi-Fi network. You then open Photos and locate and tap the AirPlay icon before selecting your Apple TV from the list. You can then begin playback.

Photo Stream

The Photo Stream pulls in photographs from a variety of sources. You are even able to take a photo on another device, such as an iPhone, and have it appear on your iPad via iCloud. The Photo Stream is also the place where imported photos from a digital camera will go. You can also sync with iPhoto on a Mac.

Indeed, iCloud is a brilliant manager of your Photo Stream and your last 1,000 photos are held. When you want to touch up photos or keep them, they just need to be saved to the Camera Roll.

Slideshows

When you take photographs, it is with the intention of viewing them later on to relive the memories for yourself, or show them off to friends and family. While you can open individual photos one by one and show people, you can also create a slideshow. This will play automatically, so people can view them without intervention.

Send an image to Photo Stream by tapping it and selecting Share, then choose Photo Stream

Rearrange albums

1 Enter Photos app To start rearranging your albums, enter the Photos app.

2 Select the Albums tab Move to the top of the screen and select the Albums tab.

3 Free the stack Long-press the selected album to free it up and then reposition it as you wish.

4 Drag the stack Drag the stack to the new location and release to drop it in that position.

Photos

Fig 3 The slideshows allow for music and snazzy visual transitions

It is possible to customise your slideshow and really make it your own by adding transitions and background music (Fig 3). All you have to do is open up the Photos app and tap the Photos tab. Then tap Slideshow. You can select to turn Music on and find a piece to play from the music that is stored on your device. You can also choose your preferred slide transitions, ranging from visual dissolves to origami effects. These will give your slideshow an interesting and more polished feel.

When you have finished, simply tap Start Slideshow and it will begin to play all of the photos in your Camera Roll from the start. You can open specific albums and play images from there if you want a more targeted slideshow. This is great for showcasing your holiday snaps, for instance.

Share
The Share option not only lets you send images to social media and email but also to a printer. You can use it as wallpaper and even assign it to a contact

Edit
The Edit option allows you to manipulate your images in a variety of ways in order to enhance them

Options
Once you've tapped the Share button, you can share the photo via many different ways, including assigning it to a contact

Slideshow
Tapping on Slideshow will bring up a slideshow of your images, taking every picture from an album

Use the built-in grid guidelines when you are cropping to centre your photograph perfectly

Edit your photos

Are your shots looking a little shabby? Do they need a bit of a lift? You can easily make simple and subtle enhancements from within your Photos app to really make your favourite images shine.

To get started with your editing, open up a photograph and tap Edit at the top of the screen. This will then take you to the editing mode, which offers you simple-yet-effective techniques to enhance your images. The features available range from rotation to enhance, red-eye removal and crop.

Pressing rotate will flip your image by 90 degrees. Keep tapping to rotate it back to the original image. The enhance option automatically scans your photo and then adds an effect which gives it greater depth and colour. For example, a washed-out image can be made more vivid. Red-eye reduction asks you to tap each eye. It will then remove any redness from it. And finally, Crop places a series of lines across your image and allows you to trim away the excess for a perfectly composed capture.

By using these techniques, you will be able to make some small alterations to your photographs that can make a big difference to their appearance. Images are then saved to your Camera Roll.

Make photos instantly better

1 Find an image Locate and select a photograph that you would like to apply edits to.

2 Tap Enhance Tapping Enhance will give your photo an automatic lift, for pleasing results.

Use the Shared Photo Streams feature

1 Find Photo Stream Tap the Photo Stream option (the centre tab at the top of the screen).

2 Add a stream Tap the + icon in the top-left of the screen to call up a window.

3 Fill in details In the To entry box, type the iCloud email of the person you are sharing with.

4 Create Tap Create and a new album appears. Open the album and tap Add Photos.

Photo Booth

Photo Booth

Why stick to taking boring, simple snaps when you can have some creative fun and jazz them up?

You'll use it to...

Make fun images
Select from a host of effects

Share pictures
Send your snaps to others

Share on social media
Facebook and Twitter photographs

Edit photographs
Use your fingers to fine tune

Distort images
From mirror to X-ray

Take normal shots
Opt for a sensible approach

Make photos more fun

With the Photo Booth app, you can take photographs on your iPad with a whole host of effects (Fig 1). From light tunnels to twirl, squeeze and stretch, you can use either the front-facing or back-facing cameras. When you are finished, it's really easy to share your newly created images with your friends and family.

Use and manipulate creative photo effects

Browse through the list of effects and then select the one that you want to use when taking your photograph. You can choose from a thermal camera, mirror, X-ray, kaleidoscope, normal, light tunnel, squeeze, twirl and stretch (Fig 2).

When you make your choice, you will then be given control over the camera. In the left corner of the screen, you can go back and select a different effect from the one that will now be showing. Or you can tap the camera icon, in which case a photograph will

Fig 1 (above) There are loads of different effects to choose from

Fig 2 (right) Here we see Photo Booth's kaleidoscope photo effect in action – try it out for great results!

be taken. Move the iPad around in order to change the effect and use your fingers to manipulate the image. Not all images can be manipulated, but some effects, such as kaleidoscope, give you some control over the finished result.

The images are placed in the Camera Roll in the Photos app but they will also be available to view via Photo Booth. The whole idea is that you have a lot of fun producing your images, so don't be afraid to experiment and try to push the boundaries to see what sort of effects you can produce.

Share images through email

Press the Share button in the bottom right-hand corner of the screen and you will be prompted to select the photographs you have taken via the app. Tap on the images you want, which will highlight the Email option. By tapping on Email, the Email app will open on the iPad and the picture will be embedded within a message. Simply compose your email message as you would normally and then hit Send to show off your Photo Booth masterpiece to everyone you know.

Share on social networks

You can also select Copy when you press the Share button and then choose a photo. This handy feature will let you paste the image within another app. As mentioned previously, the images you take with Photo Booth are saved to your Photos app. By opening this and selecting an image, you are able to press the Share button and send it to a whole host of different services, including the social networks Facebook and Twitter.

By tapping the icon in the bottom-right corner, you can switch from front to rear-facing cameras

Edit by touching

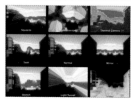

1 Take a photo Select an effect and then point the camera at your subject.

2 Use your fingers Depending on the effect, use your fingers to start manipulating the image.

3 Twist and turn Experiment with what you can do, twisting and turning your fingers around.

4 Tilt and touch Tilt the iPad around, pinch your fingers and see what results you get.

Game Center

Get social and allow others in on the action when you're playing games on your iPad

You'll use it to…

Compete against others
Invite people to join in your games

Expand your network
Be more social with multiplayer

Get going quickly
All you need is your Apple ID

Assign email addresses
Let people find you with ease

Stay connected all the time
Sign in and you're in the game

Climb the leaderboards
See how your score ranks against friends

Play games with friends

The Game Center app is the hub of your gaming life on your iPad. You can use it to invite others to join you in multiplayer games and you can also compare your score with others people to see how your skills rank against the best. There is an auto-matching facility too which lets you hook up with other gamers around the world.

Set up Game Center

As long as you are running iOS 4.1 or later, you will see the Game Center icon on your Home Screen. When you tap on this, the Game Center will open and it will ask you if it can send Push Notifications. This means it will inform you of any gaming details relevant to the titles you are playing. You can choose yes at this stage and, if you decide later you don't want it, just turn it off via the Settings app.

To log in to Games Center, input your Apple ID password when you are prompted (Fig 1), and tell the app where you reside and

Fig 1 (above) The Game Center app is the place to go on your iPad for multiplayer gaming and challenges

Fig 2 (right) Your profile will be the first you see after logging in

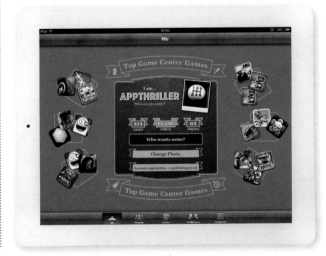

your date of birth. This information is intended to prevent under-age play of certain game titles which have age restrictions. Once you have entered this info, confirm the terms and conditions, choose a Nickname to be identified by and you can also add another email if you like. For every email address that you add, you will be sent a message and asked to confirm the address via an internal link.

At this stage, you are in the Game Center and ready to go (Fig 2). All you have to do next is add a few gaming friends to play against.

Game Center friends

Select the Requests icon within the Game Center app. It will now allow you look for friends which you can do via their Nickname if you know it or you can also use their email address. The app lets you write a message to them as part of the invite and it's worth doing this so that your friend knows that it is really from you. Of course, you will not only be seeking friends. They will look for

you too. Requests will appear in the app if they've approached by Nickname or via email if an email address is used.

Achievements

The Games page shows all of the games you have that are Game Center-compatible. To access your Achievements, tap on a game. This will show what can be earned within each title and it will also have a description and a point value – the higher the number of points, the better you will look.

Achievements give you some bragging rights since you can compare your points with those of friends, creating a friendly and competitive spirit.

If you want to create a fresh Apple ID, this is easy to do on the app's opening page

Find friends

1 Friends tab Tap on the 'Friends' tab that's right at the bottom of the screen to open it up.

2 Recommendations Tap the 'Recommendations' section that's above your friends list.

3 Review recommendations Find someone you know and tap on 'Send Friend Request'.

4 Use contacts Scroll to the bottom and tap on 'Use My Contacts' to add more friends.

Game Center

Play online

When you are all set up and ready to play, simply go to the Game Center on your iPad by tapping the icon. Once the app is open, you can do one of two things: play games against a friend or simply play on your own.

For the former option, tap on the Friends tab. Both you and your chosen gaming buddy will have to have downloaded the same game in order to play together. To see what you can play together, a list of games that you both have in common will appear under each Friend. All you have to do is tap the name of a game you want to play to send an invitation to your pal. This will let them know that you want to hook up. They will need to respond to this so you have to hang fire until they Accept or Decline your request.

Fig 3 By tapping on an achievement, you can send your friends a challenge

Invite
When you are ready to invite friends to play, all you need to do is tap on the Friends icon in order to be taken to the various options

Leaderboards
The aim is to amass a load of points so that you can be the king of gaming and you can see where you fall on the leaderboard

Status
You can change your photo and declare whether you are ready for action or not by tapping the bottom icon to the far left

Games
Games can be chosen by tapping on the Games icon. You will then be able to see the games that you have in common with your friends

Once you add friends to Game Center, their scores will appear in the left-hand column

When they accept it the game begins, so tap Play. You will now accumulate points. As we've said, you can also play alone, in which case you'll just tap the name of the game. When finished, tap Done to end. You can even challenge friends for achievments (Fig 3).

Leaderboards

When you select a game, you will be able to see your ranking and achievements within that game, if they exist. You will also be able to see the leaderboards and these show stat tables for that day as well as for the week and an all-time tally. You can tap on the name of a player and this will show their statistics and where they lie in the gaming scheme of things.

Once you've found out who is the reigning champion of a particular game, you are able to send them a friend request by tapping on their name. You can also send them a challenge via the same pop-up window. Not all leaderboards are the same and they depend on the game that you have selected. The idea is generally the same though, and the leaderboards are a wonderful way to foster a competitive spirit and show the progress that you and your friends are making.

Finding leaderboards

1 View tables Tap Games, select a game title and then press the Leaderboard tab.

2 Different days You will now see the leaderboards for today, this week and all time.

Edit your status

1 It's Me Tap on the Me tab and you will see your account page with all your details.

2 Tap status In order to alter you gaming status, tap within the Status box.

3 Keyboard Use the keyboard to input your status and tap Done when finished.

4 Add photo While you're here, you may as well add a photo. Tap Add Photo to insert a pic.

Newsstand

Never darken the door of a newsagent again with magazines direct to your iPad

You'll use it to...

Buy newspapers
Read through many national papers

Subscribe to magazines
Get a subscription to your favourite mag

Enjoy interactivity
Play with video and audio

Get free issues
Enjoy a trial issue of many publications

Rate publications
Tell publishers what you think

Navigate with ease
Flick through mags as you would a real one

Read thousands of magazines on the go

With Newsstand, you can enjoy subscriptions to your favourite magazines and newspapers and even have new issues automatically download to your iPad. There are thousands of publications out there to suit all tastes and pockets, and there are sometimes freebies to be had, too.

The Newsstand Store

When you open the Newsstand app for the very first time, you will see a set of empty shelves. These will obviously need filling! To do this, in the top right-hand corner, you will see the 'Store' button. Tap on this and you will be taken to the front end of Apple's Newsstand Store where you can see what is new and noteworthy, what's hot and a slider that shows you flagged-up content (Fig 1). Browsing the Newsstand Store, you'll soon see that there is a lot to choose from. At the top of the screen, there are four options. You can see

Fig 1 (above) The Newsstand store front end gives you a great flavour of the publications on offer

Fig 2 (right) All Newsstand apps are listed here in three columns (when in landscape), which you can scroll through

All Categories, Games, Education and More. Tapping on these will take you to other parts of the App Store. To view more publications, tap on See All next to the various categories on the right-hand side of the iPad screen. This will then list all of the magazines or papers of interest to you in columns (Fig 2). The thumbnail shows the front cover of the publication and tapping on one brings up a window for a closer look on what's on offer inside that particular publication.

Buy a magazine

In order to buy a magazine or paper from Newsstand, tap on the thumbnail of the publication you want and read the details as well as ratings and reviews before deciding if you wish to install it. If you do, tap Install and the app will download. The app will appear within Newsstand. To open the publication, tap on the thumbnail. Each app operates in its own way but there will be an opportunity to buy individual issues with most of them. Tap the price and the issue will download.

Subscribe to a magazine

To subscribe, look for the subscription option in the magazine app. There may be different levels of subscription, so choose the most suitable. Once you've done this, you can ask the app to automatically push the magazines to your iPad so you never miss an issue.

You are then able to launch new issues of magazines or papers in the Newsstand folder when they're delivered. The app will also alert you when new issues are available. To manage your subscriptions, go to Settings, then 'iTunes & App Stores'. Tap 'View Apple ID' and scroll down to 'Manage App Subscriptions'.

Some publications have free subscriptions so keep an eye out for these great-value papers and mags

Purchase a mag

1 Download the mag
Visit the Newsstand Store and then download a magazine app.

2 Launch the app
Launch Newsstand and then tap on the cover of the magazine.

3 Browse issues
From within the app, browse through the issues and tap one.

4 Tap to buy
Tap 'Buy' to purchase and download the magazine.

Newsstand

Fig 3 You can use the thumbnail view at the bottom to quickly navigate an issue

Read and navigate your content

To read a magazine on your iPad, tap View next to the issue you wish to look at and it will appear on your iPad screen. Just by simply moving your fingers back and forth in a sliding motion, you are able to flick from one page to another just as you would with a paper-based publication.

By tapping the screen, you will typically see a range of options. These include the ability to search through a publication, show or add bookmarks and view the list of contents for easier navigation. There will also invariably be a Share option and Settings.

At the bottom of the screen, you will be able to see the pages as thumbnails and scroll through them (Fig 3). By tapping on a page, it will open and this is a great way of flicking straight through to a

Tabs
The bottom tabs take you to the Top Charts and Featured pages, Genius function, your purchased issues and new updates

Categories
By tapping All Categories, you can view more publications according to whether they are new, popular or featured

Information
When you tap on the title of a publication, you will see an information box which gives you extra details, ratings and reviews and related info

Open
If you already have a magazine installed on your machine, then tapping on Open will call it up. Otherwise this button will allow you to buy the publication

Tilt the iPad on its side and, in many cases, you can view extra magazine features in widescreen

section without having to keep swiping left and right to find it. If you need to see more detail on a page then simply use two fingers to pinch and pull. This will zoom in and out.

Interactive magazines

Interactive magazines go much further than the simple recreations of a printed page on an iPad. They add extra multimedia content to a magazine, whether it be a video embedded on to a page which can be called up with a simple tap or an animated infographic in which the component parts come to life when you tap or manipulate them. It brings a whole new dimension to a magazine and really showcases the ability of publications on an iPad.

Having audio included with your favourite magazine, for example, can allow you to listen to snippets of an interview as well as read about the subject matter. The beauty of this feature is that such publications are continuing to evolve and take advantage of the possibilities of an iPad. Even if it is something as simple as links to other websites, that is classed as an interactive magazine. This greatly enhances your magazine experience and enables you to get much more for your subscription money.

Using interactive content

1 Playing videos Simply tap on a video within an interactive mag and the content comes alive.

2 All sorts It's not uncommon for publications to include interactive games – tap the screen to play.

Turn automatic downloads on/off

1 Go to the Settings Navigate to the Settings app and choose 'iTunes and App Stores'.

2 Tap Apple ID Tap on your Apple ID, which you will see in the right-hand panel.

3 Input password You will be asked to input your Apple ID password, so type this in now.

4 Turn it off Select Manage under Subscriptions and turn Auto-Renewal off.

You'll use it to…

Buy books
Access the iBooks Store

Read fiction
Flick through thousands of novels

Download textbooks
Become more educated

Save your PDFs
Place PDFs in iBooks

Search through books
Find specific terms in books

Enlarge text
Make books comfortable to read

iBooks

Enjoy a good read without having to trek to the library, and save some trees at the same time

Read books on your iPad

Using iBooks, you can not only browse books and buy them in the iBookstore, you can also read them on your iPad and take advantage of great search facilities. The app puts an entire library of books at your fingertips (Fig 1).

The iBookstore

The iBookstore is the place to go to choose from thousands of books to buy and download to your iPad. The store is packed with all kinds of different genres, both fiction to nonfiction (Fig 2). You can access the iBookstore by going to the iBooks app and choosing Store in the top left-hand corner. Ensure you are connected to the internet and the iBookstore will bring up the home page which shows a selection of books on sale as well as any promotional offers.

You can search the store using the search facility in the top-right of the screen or you can select the categories which run across the

Fig 1 (above) The iBooks app comes with *Winnie The Pooh* built in

Fig 2 (right) The iBookstore is packed with all kinds of books, so you will be spoiled for choice when browsing the digital shelves

top to narrow down your search. You can also see the top charts, top authors and any books you have purchased. If you have another iOS device and you buy a book from the iBookstore on it, you can have the book download to your iPad at no extra cost. You can see these in the Not on this iPad section of the Purchased tab.

Sample/buy a book

To buy a book, search for the one you want and then tap it. An information page will appear showing you the book description, ratings and reviews and any related books. Standard book information is also shown.

As well as being able to share the information via Mail, Twitter and Facebook and even copy the link, you have two choices. You can sample the book or buy it. Tapping Sample downloads a small section of the book to your iPad for you to read. Tapping the price will prompt you for your Apple ID and this will then download the whole book to your iPad.

Navigate an ebook

When you are in your iBooks Library, simply tap on a book you want to read and it will open. By flicking your fingers left and right you are able to go back and forth between the pages. You will also see series of dots at the bottom of the screen. This lets you jump directly to a page, the number of which will be displayed below.

At the top of the screen, you will see more options. These include the ability to go back to your Library or select one of the book's chapters. You can adjust the text size and search for certain words and phrases but, handily, using the right-most icon, you can bookmark pages too.

To view a book in full screen mode, select the font button, tap Theme and select Full Screen

Search in a book

1 Tap the magnifying glass
While reading, tap the magnifying glass icon in the top-right corner.

2 Start typing
In the search field, type in words or page numbers then hit 'Search'.

3 Look up word definitions
Also, type in a word and then tap 'Search Web' or 'Search Wikipedia'.

4 Get informed
Within seconds you'll jump straight to the requested info.

Read attachments from Mail

When you receive an email with a PDF or ePub attachment, it's possible to send it to iBooks for storage and to read (Fig 3). Simply tap on the PDF and it will open up for you to read. Tap on the Share button in the top right-hand corner, however, and you will be presented with more options for what to do with the file. As well as being able to send it via Mail or print it, you will also be able to Open your PDF in iBooks. Tap on this option and the iBooks app will activate automatically.

Your PDF or ePub file will then be displayed in iBooks and become part of your iBooks library. This allows you to search through it, send it by email and print, produce notes and keep it safe for future reference.

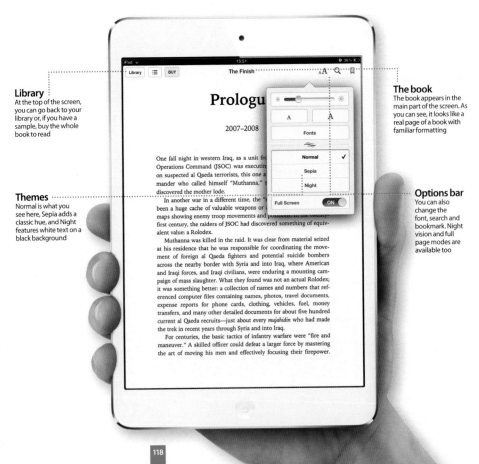

Library
At the top of the screen, you can go back to your library or, if you have a sample, buy the whole book to read

The book
The book appears in the main part of the screen. As you can see, it looks like a real page of a book with familiar formatting

Themes
Normal is what you see here, Sepia adds a classic hue, and Night features white text on a black background

Options bar
You can also change the font, search and bookmark. Night vision and full page modes are available too

To remove a highlight, select the word or phrase and use the red line icon to delete

To find PDFs in iBooks, tap on the Collections button at the top of the screen and select PDFs. A list of PDFs on your iPad will show together with a thumbnail of the file.

Annotate and make notes

You can annotate and make notes on an iBook. This is great if you are reading a textbook or educational paper, for instance, as you will be able to highlight certain parts of it and make references which will undoubtedly be a big help with your work and future revision. But even when you're reading a relaxing novel, whenever you need to have this facility it will be there.

Accessing it is easy and is a case of highlighting a word by pressing on it and then using the blue circles to expand the phrase. A selection of options appears on the screen and you can make your choice. Any notes and annotations you make are automatically saved to the book so that you can keep coming back to it for reference without worrying that they have disappeared.

As well as the ability to annotate and make notes, you can also search the text for identical words or phrases which may help you with further comments.

How to take notes

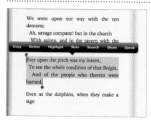

1 Select Tap, hold and drag on a word or phrase and then make a choice between Highlight and Note.

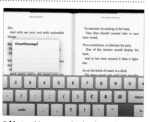

2 Notes Now use the keyboard to write a comment for a note on your selected passage.

Add a bookmark

1 Find a page When you are on a page you want to bookmark, tap the icon in the top right.

2 Red bookmark A bookmark will mark your page and this will remain when you come back.

3 View bookmarks To see your bookmarks, tap the chapter button and select Bookmarks.

4 Remove bookmark To remove a bookmark, simply tap on the red marker and it will disappear.

Pages

Get creative using Pages and put together some truly complex and visually enticing documents

You'll use it to…

Write countless letters
Send perfectly formatted letters to friends and family in any style you like

Make flyers
Make posters, artistic flyers and other eye-catching documents in a few taps

Use notes
Utilise footnotes, endnotes and take advantage of great word-count features

Share your work
Once you're finished, you can easily share your creations via many different services

Export your documents
Export your documents in various different formats for ultimate compatibility

Use the templates
Create visually impressive work by using one of the included templates

A word processor on iPad

Pages is a fully featured word processor which includes many attributes and full compatibility with the popular document formats (Fig 1). Everything you need is built in to a wonderfully clean interface. You can get Pages for £6.99/$9.99 from the App Store.

Create invitations & reports

One feature included in the Pages app that almost no other word processor includes is the ability to create flyers, and to do so with a minimum of fuss. From the moment you open the app you are presented with a selection of templates, but you can also make one from scratch.

To make a flyer or an invitation, tap the + button at the top and select Create Document. Select Blank and a blank page to work on will appear. You can now type your message and hit the paintbrush to change the fonts and colours (Fig 2).

Fig 1 (above) Pages is the ultimate word-processing solution for any iPad user

Fig 2 (right) Flyers and reports take minutes to create and can be a highly professional-looking addition to a business

Any images you find in Safari can be saved to your Camera Roll and then pasted into Pages. You can now manipulate them by touch alone which will let you change the size of each image and even change the angle at which they are presented.

Reports are created similarly. You can copy rows and columns directly from the Numbers app or by hitting the + icon and embedding charts and tables directly into your report document. The possibilities are endless.

Work with the Apple-designed templates

The great templates that Apple has included in Pages are designed for you to manipulate however you wish.

Tap the + button on the front screen and then Create Document. Now select one of the templates that fit your project. Once you've chosen a template to use, you can tap any of the text and replace it with your own and even replace any image with one that you would prefer to use. You can also move the images anywhere on the document and the text will automatically re-flow around it.

AirPrint

Apple's AirPrint function is utilised in Pages to let you share any document you create straight away with an AirPrint-enabled printer. All you need to do is tap the spanner at the top of the screen and then select Share and Print.

Now choose Print and then tap the Printer option in the next screen. The iPad will now search for a suitable printer and give you the option to print it immediately. No wires, no fuss and the most efficient printing experience imaginable.

Use the '+' icon at the top to add in some different media, tables and shapes to your documents

Find and replace

1 Use the spanner Tap the spanner in a document and then select Find from the list.

2 Tap the arrow A box will appear at the bottom. Tap the cog to the left of it.

3 Time to type Select Find and Replace – type a word to find and one to replace it with.

4 Time to replace Now choose Replace or Replace All as required then you're done.

Pages

Come to our fireworks party!

Free admission and free food.

Fig 3 Images in Pages can be manipulated very easily by touch alone

Working with images

Dealing with images when you're working in Pages is as natural as you could hope for. It almost feels futuristic once you have learned how to manipulate them to your desires.

Any image can be imported into Pages by simply copying it from your Camera Roll or saving it from the web first and then copying and pasting it. You can also tap the + icon when in a document and choose Media to copy any image in your iPad photo library to the document. It will be placed full-size in the document and so may look out of place at first, but this is where the magic happens.

Tap on the image in the document and you'll notice the blue dots around it; if you hold and pull any of them you can resize the image by touch alone to see what fits best. Using a finger and

Styles
You can choose from multiple fonts and many style options for your text

Multiple settings
Many settings are available behind the spanner including document setup and sharing options

Images
Images can be managed in any way you like and moved around the document with ease

Inserting media
Photos, tables, charts and shapes can all be inserted into a document with just a couple of taps

Via the settings, you can very easily set up your document header, footer and paper size

thumb you can rotate the image in any way and then move it into the exact position you want by simply sliding it. It really is incredibly easy to work with your images in Pages (Fig 3).

Share your documents

You can share your documents easily in Pages and the process is as simple as everything else you will encounter in this superb app. Tap the spanner icon at the top and then check the various options available to you.

You can email the document and choose which format you want to send it in (PDF, Word or Pages) and then fill in the recipient's email address. The title of the document will form the title of the email so most of the work is already done for you.

You can also copy the document to iTunes for safekeeping or to a WebDAV account by selecting the appropriate option. Remember that if you enabled iCloud when you first ran the app, all of your documents will be automatically stored online for you and are available whenever you need them. There are multiple sharing options and they are all easy to use, so the only thing that you need to do is decide which one to take advantage of.

Open a Pages document in another app

1 Get sharing With your document open, tap the spanner icon and then hit Share and Print.

2 Another app Choose Open in Another App, your preferred format and then the app you want.

Export to .doc

1 Find the document Go to the main document screen then tap and hold the document.

2 Tap the arrow Tap the share icon at the top and then choose any option.

3 Time to convert Choose Word from the next screen and the document will start converting.

4 It's exported The file will now be saved in .doc format ready for you to share.

Numbers

Numbers is Apple's answer to Microsoft Excel, and you'll find that it succeeds in all the important areas

You'll use it to…

Use clever templates
Build spreadsheets for multiple tasks using the useful built-in templates

Add complex calculations
Take advantage of more than 250 useful functions so Numbers does the thinking

Include your media
Insert photos and videos into all of your spreadsheets to enhance the experience

Share your work
Share your creations with your friends and colleagues in mere seconds

Undo mistakes
You can undo your errors even after a spreadsheet has been closed

Build tables
Build tables and use charts to manage your data and stay on top of your workload

Present facts and figures in style

You can present all of your numbers and data in styles that are easily understood by others using Numbers (Fig 1). The prebuilt charts and tables make organising information as easy as can be within a spreadsheet. It's downloadable from the App Store for £6.99/$9.99.

Create a spreadsheet

The process for creating a new spreadsheet in Numbers could not be simpler. However, there are a few choices open to you when you are getting started.

The front screen will show a Getting Started spreadsheet and a + button at the top. Tap the + and you will be presented with the option to create a spreadsheet. Choose this and a selection of templates will appear on screen (Fig 2). If you choose the blank template you will be given a completely blank canvas to work with, but think about the task you want to complete before choosing

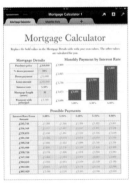

Fig 1 (above) **Numbers can handle presenting complex data in a natural way that appeals to everyone**

Fig 2 (right) **You can create new spreadsheets in Numbers in seconds**

this and have a look at the templates that are available, just in case a different one will be more suitable. Whatever template you decide upon, simply tap a thumbnailed spreadsheet and it will fill the screen ready for you to work on. You can now tap on any cell or pinch to make the rows and columns larger and interact with every single part of the new spreadsheet. You'll soon come to realise that creating a new spreadsheet in Numbers is incredibly efficient.

Intelligent tables

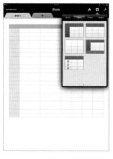

The tables built into Numbers are incredibly useful when building new spreadsheets. Tap the + icon at the top when in a spreadsheet and then choose Tables from the top bar.

You will now be able to choose from six screens of tables, each containing five choices in different colours and with specific uses. Some have checkboxes built-in and others are plain and simple which could be useful for presenting simplistic data. Thirty intelligent tables makes Numbers even more useful.

Sharing your spreadsheets

When you have finished creating your spreadsheet, sharing it couldn't be simpler. Simply head back to the main screen where all of your files are held and hold your finger down on one of them.

The sharing icon (a curved arrow) will appear at the top and tapping this will bring up options to email the spreadsheet, open it in another app, copy to iTunes or copy to WebDav. You then need to choose the format to share it in and the sharing will be completed. You can share spreadsheets in just four taps which is ideal for fast, seamless file transfers.

You can choose as many files as you like to share at once by simply tapping on each one

Make a 3D chart

1 Locate the charts Tap the + icon at the top when in a spreadsheet and select Charts.

2 Go to 3D Tap 3D and then choose a chart style that you want to use.

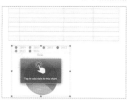

3 A simple tap Tap the chart as soon as it's placed in your current spreadsheet.

4 Choose your data Highlight some cells and the data will be added to the chart.

Numbers

Fig 3 A huge number of functions and formulas are easily accessible when you need them

Functions and formulas

You have more than 250 functions and formulas at your disposal in Numbers and dealing with so many options is not usually easy on any mobile device. However, the combination of the iPad screen and clever software implementation make accessing, learning and using them really easy.

To use a specific function, tap any cell and then tap the '=' sign at the top of the keyboard. The keyboard will change and you will see a Functions button over to the right. Tap this button and a list of functions will appear which you can select from and immediately add to the cell. If you tap the blue arrow to the right of the function name, you will be able to read a full description of what the function does and how it can be used.

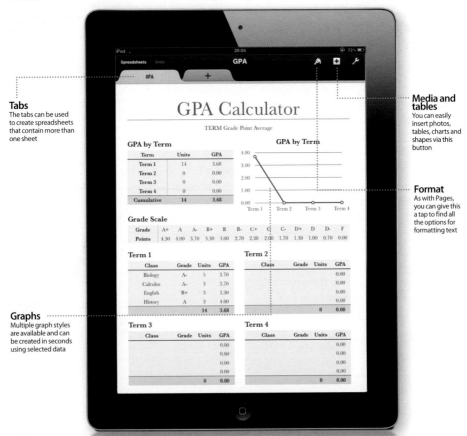

Tabs
The tabs can be used to create spreadsheets that contain more than one sheet

Media and tables
You can easily insert photos, tables, charts and shapes via this button

Format
As with Pages, you can give this a tap to find all the options for formatting text

Graphs
Multiple graph styles are available and can be created in seconds using selected data

When you double-tap a cell, note the way the keyboard changes and the shortcuts on offer

You can also tap the Categories option at the bottom to access many more useful functions. Formulas are also input through the = sign at which point the keyboard will offer many shortcuts to commonly used functionality. You will need to input instructions manually, but a range of formulas are available to select.

Sliders, steppers and pop-ups

Some functionality within Numbers is designed to speed up data entry and to also ensure that the inputted data is correct.

Sliders are available by selecting a cell, or a range of cells, and then tapping the paintbrush at the top. Choose Format and scroll down to Slider and press the blue arrow. You can now choose the maximum and minimum values and the increments. When you next tap the cell you can adjust the value by simply sliding along the slider that pops up.

Steppers are available in the same screen and once you have input your increments, you can change the values by tapping buttons rather than sliding. Pop-up menus are available from the Format screen too, but are designed to bring up menus when you tap a cell rather than let you input specific data.

Create pop-up menus

1 Find the function Tap the paintbrush when in a cell, select Format and then Pop-up Menu.

2 Add your items Input any text you like and the menu will appear when the cell is double-tapped.

Export to .xls

1 Choose the file Choose a file to export by holding your finger down on it.

2 Time to share Tap the sharing icon at the top and choose your sharing method.

3 Choose Excel Now choose Excel from the options that appear in the next screen.

4 The conversion process The file will now convert to Excel ready for sharing.

The apps | Keynote

Keynote

Keynote makes presentation creation easier than ever before and the results are always impressive

You'll use it to…

Use the templates
Create superb presentations using the professionally designed templates

Share your work
Export your work in various different formats for maximum compatibility

Use media
Insert engaging media anywhere in your presentation to bring your work to life

Animate away
Animate aspects of each slide – an ideal way to keep the audience's attention

Control your presentation
Swipe, flick and tap your presentation to control it wirelessly with your iPad

Keep your work safe
Use iCloud to keep all of your precious work safe, no matter which device you use

Create presentations

Keynote can help you to create sophisticated presentations in mere minutes (Fig 1). You can use the templates or start from scratch, but the end result is almost always exactly what you wish for. Download it from the App Store for £6.99/$9.99.

Make a slideshow

To make your first slideshow using Keynote, open the app on your iPad and then start by tapping the + icon at the top of the interface. Then select Create Presentation. Browse through the options and choose a simple template such as White or Black and you will be presented with a slide showing an example photo and some text (Fig 2). Double-tap the large text and replace it with your own words and do the same with the smaller text. You can add whatever you like to the first slide and then tap the + icon in the bottom left-hand side of the screen.

Fig 1 (above) The complexity of Keynote is masked by the intuitive and simplistic touch interface

Fig 2 (right) Creating long and complex slideshows feels very natural when you first use Keynote

A new window will pop up and you can select a another slide type to insert. Once you have chosen one to use, it will fill the main section and be shown as a thumbnail in the left-hand panel. As you add in new slides to your presentation you can hold each thumbnail and drag it to a new position – you can move your slides about in any way you like.

Choosing and managing the individual slides is a very easy process. You'll find that most of your time will be spent writing and adding your content to each one, to make your presentation as exciting as possible.

Flick, tap and drag to navigate your presentation

Holding your finger on a slide thumbnail will select it – you can now drag it to a new position in the slide timeline to change the order.

Tapping an individual slide will display it in full on the right-hand side for editing and this will help you to decide exactly where in the presentation each slide should be placed. If you have many slides, simply flick up and down the thumbnails to see slides that are off the screen.

Share your presentation

After you're finished creating, sharing a presentation takes only a few seconds. When in a presentation, tap the spanner at the top and then choose Share and Print. You can now choose to email it or open it in another app. You can also copy it to iTunes or to WebDAV for safe keeping, but there are more than enough options for most people to share their work in any way they like. When exporting, an option will pop up to choose which exact format the presentation should be shared in.

You can delete individual slides by holding your finger down and using the pop-up menu

Add animations

1 Use the spanner Tap the spanner at the top and select Transitions and Builds.

2 Useful pop-ups A self-explanatory pop-up will appear. Dismiss it.

3 Obvious indicators Tap on a slide and then the tap the pop-up icon next to it.

4 Choose your animation Now select the type of animation you want and the timing.

Presenter notes

When making a presentation, it is all too easy to just read what is on the screen to the audience. We have all seen this happen, but it makes for a poor experience and one that offers little extra information for everyone concerned.

Being able to talk about a subject at length, or some figures on screen for example, will make all of the difference to making a presentation effective, interesting and worth the time it takes to create it. You can carry notes with you or you can use your iPad properly and keep the notes stored on it next to each slide so that the talk fits perfectly with the visuals.

When in a slide, tap the spanner icon and select Presenter Notes. Now type in some notes that are applicable to that slide, such as

Fig 3 **Make your presentation flow by using the built-in notes feature to keep you talking**

The notes
Presenter Notes will be crucial when the time comes to make the presentation

Media
Images, shapes and charts can be included in any slide with ease

Thumbnails
The thumbnail column helps to create presentations in perfect order

Animated content
You can use a variety of animations in your presentations to gain more interest

Presenter notes will be shown to everyone if you have it enabled when mirroring

extra information or description as to what the slide shows. Repeat this for each slide in the set. When you are making the presentation, go back to Presenter Notes mode and as each slide is displayed to the audience, you can refer to your notes throughout (Fig 3). It's so simple, but extremely effective.

Video mirroring

The iPad comes with the ability to mirror its screen on compatible equipment and this can be used for presenting as well as for watching movies and playing games. The process to mirror your presentation is very quick, as is shown in the related step-by-step, and the advantages are numerous.

For starters, you can see what is on your iPad screen at any time and be certain that the audience is viewing the same slide which is reassuring. The main benefit, however, is that you can use the iPad as a controller and having such a large screen to manage your slides is infinitely more useful than a traditional remote control.

The iPad can create a presentation, store notes, wirelessly deliver your work and even control the presentation as it happens. This highlights just how useful Keynote can be.

Add presenter notes

1 Spanner button Tap the Spanner button in the top right and then 'Presenter Notes'.

2 Type your notes in The on-screen keyboard will appear, so use this to type your notes.

Use the slide navigator cameras

1 Touch and drag
Touch and hold a slide until it rises and then drag it to the right.

2 Select your slides
While still holding the first slide, tap the others you want to move.

3 Select location
Drag the set to the desired location within the slide navigator.

4 Secure position
When you've positioned the set of slides, just take your finger off.

GarageBand

GarageBand is a recording studio in your pocket with the ability to recreate instruments perfectly

You'll use it to…

Remember new tunes
If you suddenly think of a new tune or chord you can capture it immediately

Play new instruments
Play any instrument from a vast number of offerings for a symphony of sounds

Use your own equipment
Attach your own instruments and then play and record them instantly

Keep in sync
A great way to manage all of your songs automatically using the iCloud

Mix and match
Mix many instruments and sounds into one multilayered song for amazing results

Jam with friends
Play along with friends using wireless connections and make music together

Music made easy

GarageBand is capable of acting as a mini recording studio for all of your instruments. You can play many of the included instruments on the app or simply plug your own in for added realism. It's downloadable from the App Store for £2.99/$4.99.

Create a song

Creating a song in GarageBand is as simple as doing so with real musical instruments. The interface is obvious enough to let anyone jump in and start straight away (Fig 1).

Begin by choosing an instrument from the many that are available via the Instruments icon in the top bar. Once you have decided what you want to make music with, tap the red Record button at the top and start playing. You will hear a metronome in the background to help you keep time, and as soon as you are satisfied with what you've done, press Stop at the top.

Fig 1 (above) GarageBand can help you achieve all of your musical aspirations with ease

Fig 2 (right) You can layer several instrument tracks together to create a musical masterpiece

You can now play your track back to hear what it sounds like. It will be saved automatically, so you needn't worry about losing any of your musical masterpieces, and you can add further tracks (Fig 2).

Keyboards

Within the instruments section you will see an option called Keyboard. Tap this and a keyboard will immediately fill up the screen. Tap the instrument description and you will see the selected keyboard highlighted in the window that pops up. You will now see a selection of keyboards shown on the screen and a row of choices just above them. Each choice at the top includes eight instruments, making a total of 48. Experimenting with each will help you realise which one you need. Just tap a picture of a keyboard and it will fill the screen straight away with a realistic design so you know for sure which one you are using.

Drums

Within the instruments selector there are eight different drum kits to choose from. Enter the Instruments panel and select Drums to see all of the choices which range from Classic Studio Kit to a Hip Hop Drum machine. Each type of kit will produce very different sounds and so you may want to experiment with each of them before you start recording.

You can also tap the Settings spanner in the top right-hand corner to adjust the echo, reverb and all sorts of other options that can change the tone of your finished creation. On some kits you can also play around with the resonance and cutoff via the circular volume buttons at the top.

Choose Sampler from instruments to record a sound that will be played by the keyboard

Swipe and tap

1 Tap and select a track
Tap on any track in Arrangement view to select it for editing.

2 Drag and trim it
Drag the handles at either end of the track to trim the start or end.

3 Extra options
Double-tapping a track will show extra options such as Cut or Split.

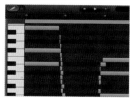

4 Open the piano roll editor
From these, tap Edit to open the advanced piano roll editor.

GarageBand

Fig 3 Smart instruments can help anyone create beautiful music wherever they are

Smart instruments

Smart instruments take the notion of music creation to a whole new level for those who do not have much experience when it comes to musical things. They are designed to let you create pitch-perfect music simply by playing around (Fig 3). However they also offer some educational bonuses to help you understand chords and the way music is put together to create a positive end result.

Go to Instruments and swipe across until you see the Smart Strings, Smart Drums, Smart Guitar, Smart Bass and Smart Keyboard. Select one of the instruments, for example Guitar, and the standard instrument panel will fill the screen. You will notice that chord names are shown above the strings – simply tap one of the names and the chord will play as if you strummed it perfectly.

Tracks
You can create multiple tracks which play alongside each other to create a big-band sound

Jamming
You can jam with other people who are also running GarageBand on iOS devices or Macs

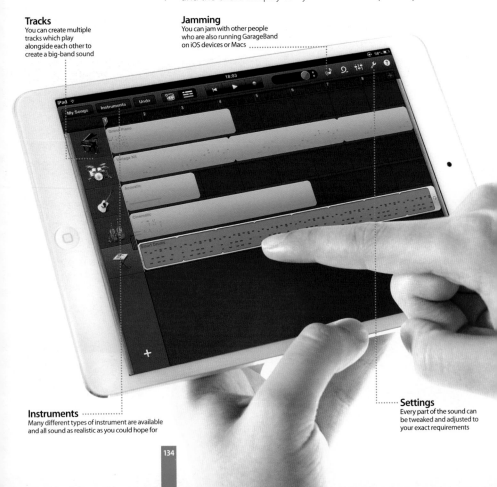

Instruments
Many different types of instrument are available and all sound as realistic as you could hope for

Settings
Every part of the sound can be tweaked and adjusted to your exact requirements

Tapping keys harder will make the sounds louder, just like when playing a real instrument

You can also tap each string in order to understand how the chord is made up. Tapping the Autoplay button at the top will let you automatically adjust the speed at which chords are played to add extra variety.

Jam Sessions

Jam sessions are invaluable to real bands and GarageBand fully caters for the interaction required when practising or laying down new tunes. The Jam Session feature is available in GarageBand by tapping the music note at the top when in an instrument panel.

You will be asked to enable Bluetooth if it is not already and then a new window will appear. You can now create a new session by tapping the button at the top which will bring up a screen showing any other band members who are within Bluetooth range or you can join a session that is already active.

Whether you are leading the session or merely playing along, the end result is the same because you really do get to jam with your friends and hear what the results sound like as they are played. The easy set up also means you can strike up a jam any time you like and create some great music with friends.

Connect to a jam

1 Begin the Jam Tap the musical note near the top of the interface to start the Jam Session.

2 Everyone's connection Make sure everyone else has Bluetooth enabled and are in range to start a jam.

Master controls

1 Drag from the left
Drag the handle next to the track icons to reveal all their controls.

2 Fix the volume mix
Each track has a volume slider, so you can mix tracks to perfection.

3 Solo the important ones
Tap the headphones icon beside a track name to listen in solo mode.

4 Mute the bad tracks
To mute a track, tap the speaker icon. It glows blue when active.

iMovie

Let your imagination run wild with iMovie and make professional, fun and unique creations every time

You'll use it to…

Build a memory
Create audio-visual records of special events

Touch your movie
Use touch to adjust every second of a movie

Take advantage of themes
Manage themes for a fantastic end product

Animate your photos
Animate every photo for seamless videos

Create a film studio
Make your films look professional

Share with friends
Share your creations in many different ways

Create & edit films

iMovie is designed to let you simply drop media including videos and photos into it and to then edit them all together. The end result is a movie format that looks as though you spent hours creating a masterpiece. In reality, you can create that masterpiece in minutes. It's downloadable from the App Store for £2.99/$4.99.

Make a movie with trailers

You may wonder how trailers can work within videos, but in iMovie the idea has been taken to a whole new level (Fig 1). To use a trailer, tap the + button in the centre of the screen and choose New Trailer from the pop-up. You will now be presented with a selection of trailers in a horizontal form that you can preview. Tap the play button on each trailer and it will start playing so that you can be sure the theme fits with the content or event you are building the movie for (Fig 2). When you have found one, tap the Create icon at

Fig 1 (above) Trailers bring lots of fun and plenty of special effects to all of your home-made movies

Fig 2 (right) You can create movies in minutes in iMovie that look remarkably professional and detailed

the top-right and a new screen will pop up for you to personalise. You can type in the name of the movie, the cast members and even credits to show at the end. You can then create a storyboard by tapping the relevant icon and when you add media it will be annotated with the topics you have input. Trailers are easy, effective and stunning to watch.

Add titles and transitions

You can add titles to any image in iMovie by selecting an image from the Camera Roll and then double-tapping it at the bottom. Now choose your title style and then type in the words in the text box that appears.

Transitions between images and videos are handled by double-tapping the small arrows between the objects and then using the scroll wheel to choose the one you want to use. It all works by using simple touches.

Film from within the app

iMovie works perfectly with media you have already captured, but you can take new photos and videos while you are in the app and add them to a new project straight away.

In the editing screen, look for the camcorder icon which is placed to the right in the centre line. Tap it and you will be taken to the normal camera screen. Notice at the bottom that you can select between film and photo. Simply make your choice and snap the media to add into your movie. Then tap Use to include it in your project immediately.

You can select transitions that range from 0.5 seconds to 2 seconds. Try to use the shorter ones for consistency

Import footage

1 Tap the button Tap the media button on the left-hand side of the centre row.

2 The media screen Select the type of media you want using the buttons at the bottom.

3 Choose an item Tap a photo or video and it will jump into your current project.

4 Import the media You can now manipulate the imported footage to your preference.

iMovie

Use iMovie themes

Themes in iMovie are much more subtle than trailers. Themes are intended to give you an environment for your movie to play within, rather than offer special effects that build around a storyline (Fig 3).

From the editing screen, tap the cog icon which is in the top right-hand corner and you will be presented with a selection of thumbnails which designate each theme available to you. Once you have chosen one that you want to use, highlight it then press Done. It will then be added to your project.

You will now need to play the movie to see what it looks like and if you are not happy, simply press the cog again and select another one. This is by far the best way to test each theme until you find the one you prefer.

Fig 3 Themes can add a great touch of personality to all of your movie creations

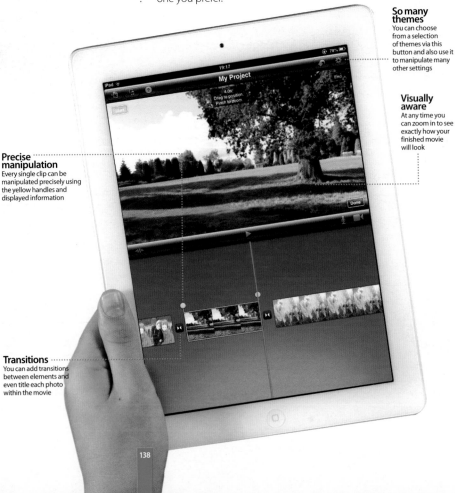

So many themes
You can choose from a selection of themes via this button and also use it to manipulate many other settings

Visually aware
At any time you can zoom in to see exactly how your finished movie will look

Precise manipulation
Every single clip can be manipulated precisely using the yellow handles and displayed information

Transitions
You can add transitions between elements and even title each photo within the movie

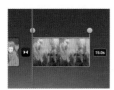

To make some precision edits, you can pinch to zoom in to each clip and examine it up close

You can also choose to use the music that is embedded in the theme, or of course you can select some music to add in from your own music library on your iPad. You will also be able to set a default fade from black or white for the entire theme in the settings screen.

The Precision Editor

The Precision Editor is extremely effective for creating professional-looking clips and it gives you a lot of control over each part of your movie, but it is not obvious how it should be used at first. The process is, however, very natural and quite easy to use once you understand the basics. It's worth taking some time to get used to it and the results will make the effort worthwhile.

All you need to do is tap on a photo or video in your timeline and then look for the yellow bars with circles at the top of them. Think of these as handles that you can drag into position because this is exactly what they are. As you move them along, you will see detailed information in the top half of the screen that lets you precisely choose how long each clip should be and where it should start and end. Play around with these precision controls to see exactly what you can achieve with this feature.

Accurate positioning

1 Grab the handle Tap and hold a yellow circle and move it. Notice the timer at the top.

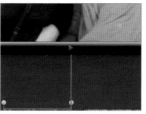

2 Back to the start You can also tap the icon to jump straight to the start of the clip.

Use sound effects

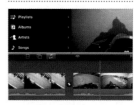

1 Tap on music icon
Tapping on the music icon brings up different sound options.

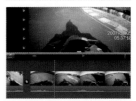

2 Navigate sound effects
Browse through the sounds to find the one that 'fits' your movie.

3 Tap to insert into timeline
In the sound menu, tap the 'play' icon to preview the effect.

4 Adjust settings
Double-tap on a sound clip to adjust volume and length.

iPhoto

iPhoto is the only photo-editing tool you will need because the feature set is so versatile

You'll use it to…

Edit your photos
Add effects to your photos and fix problems

Create journals
Build journals of special events in minutes

Share your work
Stream or share photos on social networks

Manage your collection
Pick out your best shots with touch gestures

Paint away
Paint colours and fixes over existing images

Compare your snaps
Compare photos side by side to choose

Edit and organise your photo collection

With iPhoto you can organise hundreds of photos using lots of different criteria and also compare selections to help you decide which ones to keep that look similar. It is a dream solution for anyone with a camera!

Smart browsing

Managing a photo collection that contains hundreds of photos is not easy, and finding individual snaps can be even more difficult (Fig 1). iPhoto, however, now brings all of the searching power of its desktop equivalent to the iPad which lets you search and find what you need in many different ways in seconds.

When you open iPhoto you will see a strip at the top with four icons included (Fig 2). You will need to sync your iPad with iTunes to ensure that you can use all of these, but once done you will be able to browse through your photo collection by album, individual

Fig 1 (above) Managing and editing your photo collection is much easier with iPhoto

Fig 2 (right) The top tabs allow you to jump straight to the album or event you want

photo, events and journals. This means that if you need to find a snap taken at a particular time or in one place you can find it relatively easily. The clever split-screen view helps when you open one of the categories and lets you tap individual thumbnails and see them full-screen, even while all of the other thumbnails are on display. It all works efficiently and accurately.

Multi-touch editing

It is likely that many of your photos will require some form of adjustment and this is another area that iPhoto shines in.

Select any photo and tap the Edit icon at the top to start the process. You can now use your fingers to pinch and zoom to see the full detail or to edit specific parts of each photograph via the icons found at the bottom of the screen. You can manipulate the sky, grass and any other aspect of each photo by touch alone.

The Swatch Book

One feature that is not noticeable at first is the Swatch Book. This is a handy element of iPhoto that contains a host of effects, all of which can be applied and removed with just one simple tap.

Find the effects icon at the bottom of the screen, it looks like a collection of stars, and tap it. A series of swatches will magically appear and include artistic, vintage and black-and-white tones. Choose one and you will see it settle at the bottom of the screen. Slide your finger along the swatch and the tones will change in gradients. It's a true highlight of the entire iPhoto experience.

Some tweaks are hidden behind icons, so tap on the help icon to see exactly what they do

Resize and crop

1 Find the icon Locate the crop icon in the bottom-left corner and tap it.

2 Create squares Hold your finger on the screen to bring up the crop grid.

3 Pinch to zoom You can now pinch with your fingers to change the size of the photo.

4 Choose any section It is easy to select any part of a photo to fill the frame.

iPhoto

Fig 3 The brushes let you change and improve every single part of a photo

Brushes

Perhaps the most artistic feature in iPhoto is the brush selection which can be used to spruce up and correct or hide flaws in any image. Apple has implemented brushes in such a way that it really is up to you how you use them and the built-in flexibility is huge.

When you tap the brushes icon at the bottom of the screen a selection will pop up for you to choose from (Fig 3). There are eight different choices and when you select one, you then use your finger to add that particular effect to a part of the photo.

The first choice is Repair which can be used to remove areas of the photo and this is useful if something just isn't quite right – zoom in as far as possible when using this and you can be very precise in what you remove. You can lighten specific areas, remove the

The output
You can share your photos or build journals from them, all via this small icon

Ultimate customisation
You can manually tweak every single aspect of each photo for the ultimate in customisation

Comparisons
Selecting multiple photos lets you compare them to choose the best one

Automation
Many tools in iPhoto let you automatically enhance all or parts of your photos

You can undo any changes you make with a brush by tapping the undo icon at the top

red-eye effect and soften and sharpen to your heart's content. No matter what you want to do to your photos, the brushes feature offers everything you need.

Photo Journals

The Photo Journal feature is a clever way to show your events and pictorial history to others in a pleasing and professional way. You can play around a lot with this feature and once you have created a new journal and chosen the photos to use in it, you can then move the photos around, resize them in any way you like and add titles and other aspects to bring some life to the presentation.

As an easy way to create a slide show of a holiday and to highlight the most important moments, the photo journal's features are guaranteed to work for everyone, no matter how much experience they have of photo curation.

You may also find that the journals you create will be what you look at the most in the future because of their ability to tell a story in one page much more effectively than simply browsing through a selection of photos. Creating a Photo Journal is an amazing way to preserve your most precious memories.

Create a new journal

1 Choose an event Tap the sharing button at the top and choose the Journal option.

2 The content Select the photos that you want to use and tap Create Journal. That's it – you're done!

Social media sharing

1 Sharing choices
Tap the Sharing button at the top of the screen for a list of options.

2 Flickr
Share your image to Flickr by logging into your account.

3 Twitter
Thanks to Twitter integration, you can tweet from within iPhoto.

4 Facebook
Facebook needs your permission before you can send photos to it.

145

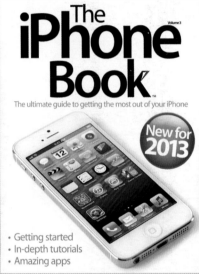
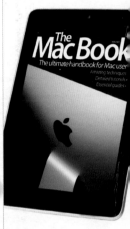